Finding Strength

How to Overcome Today

Mindy Ross

This book is dedicated to my husband, Justin, for pushing me to pursue God's plan for my life; for being my greatest encourager, the first-string parent when I needed to write, and a God-given thorn in my side when I needed an attitude adjustment. You are my home, my love, my coach—and without your support, this book may never have been written.

From twelve years old to forever and eternity—love, Me

"Finally, be strong in the Lord and in his mighty power." –Ephesians 6:10

Introduction

Hey there! I am pumped to share with you some principles and stories that I believe will empower you for the daily battle that we call life!

First off, I want you to know that this book is not written from a position of "holier than thou" but rather a position of "Dang, I know how that feels." I am just a girl who has allowed God's power (which is infinite) to be strong in my weaknesses (which are many). For a long while, it has been my goal to bring others along in this journey. Along the way, I realized that there are so many people who have what I call a "strength story" in the making—a story of struggle and victory, of valleys and mountains. I also realized that there are some common threads within these stories and key elements to helping others find their strength. So, over countless cups of coffee, I sat with these amazing people, listened to their stories, took notes, and put together the book that is in your hands today. It is a compilation of my experiences, their experiences, some prayerful insight, and practical advice on *Finding Strength*.

I have always been the type of reader to skip around and read only the parts of the books that I feel apply to me, so I wrote this book as such. I realize that when the storms of life hit, we need help quickly and cannot afford to read for weeks before getting to the part we need. So browse the chapter titles and feel free to skip around, or simply read front-to-back, whatever tickles your fancy. I encourage you to take notes in a journal along the way, so I've included some journal prompts at the end of each chapter. It is amazing how journals can help us work through our thoughts and become therapy for our souls.

Then, when you are ready, I would love to hear your strength story! You can share your story with me at my website: www.mindyross.org

It is my prayer that the principles written in these pages will comfort you, support you, encourage you, and inspire you. So, without further ado, let's begin your journey to finding strength.

Mindy Ross

Contents

Section 1

Section 2

Section 1

-1-
My Story

*Before I formed you in the womb I knew you, before you were
born I set you apart; I appointed you as a prophet to the nations.*

—Jeremiah 1:5

I grew up in a loving, Christian home, with two great parents who taught me all the most important lessons in life. I knew how to work hard, not quit, tell the truth, respect my elders, pray before meals, and most importantly, I learned that God loved me more than I would ever know.

I am the oldest of five children, which made me responsible, mature, and driven. I excelled in school and at sports. My life was pretty amazing, and I should have been grateful and happy, but around the age of fourteen, I began a battle with insecurity and anxiety that held me captive for years. On the outside, I had everyone fooled that I was confident and joyful, but on the inside, I was in what seemed like a constant battle. On the outside I had it all. I was the popular cheerleader who dated the stud quarterback, partied on the weekends, and still maintained honor roll.

Looking back, I can see why I was misunderstood. It may have appeared as if I had it all together, but that was far from the truth. You see, I wore the makeup to cover up every physical flaw, because I thought that one pimple might get me rejected from the popular crowd. I wore the cute clothes because I found acceptance in being "liked" for my looks. I gave academics and athletics my very best, because I couldn't handle failure. The thought of missing an assignment frightened me. The thought of losing, falling, or disappointing my team was terrifying. My efforts to appear "perfect" were derived from my fear of being rejected as the flawed, weak, insecure girl I really was.

Maybe you can relate to that person, or maybe I just helped you understand that girl a little better—you know, the one you love to hate. And I was hated, ridiculed, pranked, and gossiped about by people who had no idea the weight of their words and actions.

I've since forgiven them, knowing what I do now. They didn't know the real me because I never let her show.

I hoped that once high school was over, a fresh start would free me up, but the pressure to be perfect only grew after graduation.

"I remember going into the girls' bathroom and not being able to look at myself in the mirror because of the shame."

Stars and Bars

During college I made a semipro cheerleading team in Columbus, Ohio, where I was able to continue my passion for dance. I loved the rush of adrenaline that I felt standing behind the curtains as I heard the announcer calling us out to perform for crowds of thousands in the arena.

I wish I could say that I look back on that era and smile, but along with the opportunities to perform came opportunities for more parties, more fake eyelashes, big hair, skimpy uniforms, and high boots. I was "living the dream" once more—out in front, on display, the perfect girl with the perfect life. I still attended church faithfully every Sunday, but I was starting to come in more hung over, feeling more guilty and more ashamed of the person I had been on Saturday night.

My dance career began to advance. I was given opportunities to be cast for performances at high-profile Super Bowl parties, where I would meet movie stars, music idols, and NFL Hall of Famers. It was my job to ensure they all had eye candy during the parties. We danced in whatever costumes they chose for us, for however long as they asked, just to entertain the stars.

Was it fun? Of course. I bet most girls would dream of dancing with rap stars, Hollywood actors, and NFL players, but there was always this moment, amidst all the busyness of the crowds, when I would take a mental step back, looking at myself as if from a distance. I was not happy with what I saw. I remember going into the girls' bathroom and not being able to look at myself in the mirror because of the shame.

I knew that I was meant to be more than eye candy. I knew I had been made by God for a purpose so much greater than the next big party, the next big promotion, and the next step to fame. And one day, at age twenty, I hit a turning point.

"Those two pink lines turned our world upside-down and turned us right-side up."

Two Pink Lines

My boyfriend, Justin, and I were on our way to my grandmother's house in the country. I was a few days late for my monthly cycle and was starting to get worried, so to clear my mind, we stopped in a grocery store to take a pregnancy test.

I'll never forget the wave of emotion I felt when I saw two pink lines. More than that, I'll never forget the unconditional love and support Justin had for me in that moment. Rather than get upset, fearful, or run away, he held me close and said, "We are in this together."

From that moment on, life was no longer just about the two of us. Rather than run away from church out of fear of what they would say, we ran to our pastor and told him the news. He spoke the truth in love, prayed with us, and helped us make the right decisions moving forward. We rededicated our purity to God and became abstinent until marriage. I hung up my tiny cheerleading uniform, Justin got a job working for a mortgage company while finishing his degree, and we began volunteering in the church together.

They say that God will take our mistakes and turn them into testimonies, and I can attest to that. Those two pink lines turned our world upside-down and turned us right-side-up.

"I had learned to live by the grace of God and not for the applause of man."

More Than a Face in the Crowd

Talking to our pastor was our first step toward God as a couple. After that, we found courage to take on any faith-challenge sent our way. Through volunteering at church, we discovered our hearts for ministry and began the journey that would eventually lead us to launch Impact City Church. Today, Impact City is a thriving, growing ministry that is reaching those far from God and connecting them into a growing relationship with Jesus. Hundreds have given their hearts to Christ in just three years, and many more have found a church to call home. God has blessed us with three more children since Kaden: Mckenzie is eight, Isabella is six, and Temperance is also six. (She is a testimony to be told later in the book.)

As for my fears? I can't remember the last time I had an anxiety attack, praise Jesus! And what about that insecurity? I have found that there is much more to me than looks. I have God-given value: skills, talents, and passions that are worth so much more than any amount of fame. I have learned to live by the grace of God and not for the applause of man. I know that I am not perfect but a constant work in progress, and I am okay with that. I still enjoy a new sparkly outfit and a makeover once in a while, but I choose not to be defined or valued based on my outward appearance.

Some people look back at their twenties and wish they could go back. I look ahead to my future with excitement and anticipation for the next adventure God brings our way. I have no desire for that old life, because although it looked glamorous and fun, it was full of darkness. Today, I am the crazy, fun-loving mother of four wild children, wife to that same man-crush, Justin, and pastor to the greatest group of believers this side of the Mississippi.

Today my life is full of peace, joy, laughter, challenge, adventure, and best of all, the freedom to be the woman God has called me to be.

Scripture Study

For freedom that Christ has set us free. Stand firm, than, and do not let yourselves be burdened again by a yoke of slavery. —Galatians 5:1

Provide for those who grieve in Zion—to bestow on them a crown of beauty instead of ashes, the oil of joy instead of mourning, and a garment of praise instead of a spirit of despair. They will be called oaks of righteousness, a planting of the LORD for the display of his splendor.
—Isaiah 61:3

Journal Prompts

Write down three people, places, and events that have made you who you are today. Regardless of whether they had a positive or negative effect on you, they are a part of your story. Don't be ashamed of the ugly parts of your past. God can *and will* bring beauty from our ashes.

-2-
Rock Bottom

This is my prayer in the desert; when all that's within me feels dry. This is my prayer in my hunger and need, my God is the God who provides.

—*"Desert Song" by Hillsong*

*H*ave you ever been so down that lose your motivation to get back up? Maybe you feel as if you've failed in an important area of life, or even many areas. I know the feeling. There have been times in my life when I felt like such a failure that I lost all desire to try to keep up with life. It was in that deep valley, where all seemed lost, that God brought me to my knees and gave me a second chance. Rock bottom is no fun place to be, but it can be the perfect place to rebuild. I pray Jessie's story encourages you to find strength to get back up again.

"Every anxiety attack left her in fear of the next one."

Jessie's Story

As Jessie walked into her therapist's office, as she had many times before, this time she was a bit lighter on her feet. This time she had a smile on her face. This time she hadn't come for therapy but to report to her therapist that she wouldn't be needing his help any longer.

"What's your plan?" he said, confused.

"Jesus," Jessie said with a smile on her face.

"You need a plan B, Jessie."

"Nope. That's it," Jessie said, and she walked out of the office for the last time.

Months before this, Jessie had found herself at what many call "rock bottom." Her anxiety had progressed to the point where she couldn't even stay home alone. Her family scheduled shifts to babysit her in case she had another attack with the kids around. She couldn't be around crowds; she couldn't sleep, go to the grocery store, or even play with her children without fear and anxiety overcoming her.

Jessie had begun her adult life with big aspirations. She wanted to be a nurse and had been taking courses at a local college, but with just one semester remaining, she dropped out of nursing school. Every anxiety attack left her in fear of the next one, and the fear continued to build until it had taken over her life.

It was in this place of fear and desperation where Jessie cried out to God. She and her family walked into the doors of Impact City for the first time, and for the first time, she found the hope she had been longing for. Jessie prayed a sincere prayer, surrendering her life and her anxiety over to Jesus, and found a freedom she had never before experienced.

Today, it has been over a year since her last panic attack. She serves in the nursery, attends a women's group, and looks forward to every Sunday service where she can worship the God who freed her from bondage and gave her new life. She would tell you that her life is not perfect, and she still has to fight off thoughts of sadness now and then, but now, she knows she is not alone. Now, every battle she faces is God's battle. She is stronger and more joyful than ever before.

"Rock bottom is the perfect place to start building."

Rebuilding on the Rock

If you've ever been to this place many call "rock bottom," it is a very lonely place to be. Feelings of sadness, rejection, fear, anger, and guilt may seem to play on repeat in your mind, as you watch your life spiral out of control. Each battle lost seems to make way for the next, and eventually you feel as if you've lost everything and failed at life.

If this hits home, be encouraged. Rock bottom is the perfect place to start building. When there is nothing left but you and God, you are forced to build your life on the rock that is faith in Jesus, and nothing else.

When Jesus walked the earth, there was a lot of talk about who he really was and many different opinions, but when He asked Simon Peter, "Who do you say that I am?" Peter professed, "You are the Christ, the Son of the living God."

And Jesus answered him, "Blessed are you, Simon Bar-

Jonah! For flesh and blood has not revealed this to you, but my Father who is in heaven. And I tell you, you are Peter, and on this rock I will build my church, and the gates of hell shall not prevail against it."

People try to build their lives on many things: ego, desires, bank accounts, fear of rejection, need for approval and acceptance, goals, or social status. While some of these foundations may sound good on the front end, if our life is not founded on the rock that is our faith in Jesus, it is built on shaky ground. We may even do a great job of building our house on this shaky foundation, and it may look big and beautiful in the eyes of others, but when the storms of life hit, these big and beautiful houses will fall.

> *Therefore everyone who hears these words of Mine and puts them into practice is like a wise man who built his house on the rock. The rain came down, the streams rose, and the winds blew and beat against that house; yet it did not fall, because it had its foundation on the rock. But everyone who hears these words of Mine and does not put them into practice is like a foolish man who built his house on sand. The rain came down, the streams rose, and the winds blew and beat against that house, and it fell with a great crash. —Matthew 7:24–27*

"We serve a God of second, third, fourth, and fifth chances."

The good news is, we serve a God of second, third, fourth, and fifth chances. When our life falls apart, when we feel like we've lost all that is important, and we're left alone in the aftermath of our failures, it is here in this place—this rock bottom—where we find the steady foundation upon which to build the life we were meant to have from the beginning.

So, dear friend, it is time to lift your eyes, pick up a brick, and begin to rebuild, but not upon the same foundation that led you here. This time, you build upon the rock of faith in a God who overcomes, a God who saves, a God who forgives, a God who restores, a God who works miracles. This time, you build a house—a life—that will stand the test of time.

Scripture Study

So then, just as you received Christ Jesus as Lord, continue to live your lives in him, rooted and built up in him, strengthened in the faith as you were taught, and overflowing with thankfulness. – Colossians 2:6-7

Therefore, if anyone is in Christ, the new creation has come: The old has gone, the new is here! – 2 Corinthians 5:17

Journal Prompts

What have you been trying to build your life upon? If it's anything other than faith in Jesus, decide today to stop building on that foundation and begin building a new life.

What is one thing you would like to stop doing?

What is one thing you would like to start doing?

What do you need to forgive yourself of in order to move on?

-3-

Unshakable

They called the apostles in and had them flogged. Then they ordered them not to speak in the name of Jesus, and let them go. The apostles left the Sanhedrin, rejoicing because they had been counted worthy of suffering disgrace for the Name. Day after day, in the temple courts and from house to house, they never stopped teaching and proclaiming the good news that Jesus is the Messiah—Acts 5:40–42

We are called to be the type of people who soar over storms, who run and don't get tired. We are called to be the people who don't allow the trials of this life to take them out. We are more than conquerors through Him who loves us. The joy of the Lord is our strength. We can do all things through Christ…and yet…We can find ourselves ready to quit over one disagreement. Over one bad diagnosis. Over one e-mail. Over one offensive comment.

What is it that shakes you up? What gets you to say and do things you know aren't "Christian-like"? What brings out the worst in you? For me, it's not the big events—it's all the little things that build up throughout the day, that get me to the point of saying or doing something I know I shouldn't.

"I was no longer Mindy the unshakable; I had transformed into Mindy, the irritated, exhausted, and half-crazy."

Worst Day Ever (Sort Of)

I can remember one day that everything seemed to be going wrong. Have you ever had a day like that? It was as if someone was going ahead of me to ensure my day was full of misfortune, problems, and chaos. Justin was filling in for me at the parenting class I had been attending, so I was home with our four children, one of whom had gotten to the point that he needed to see a doctor. (I have a tendency to put off doctor visits, knowing, as a nurse, that many illnesses can be fought off naturally.) So with Justin unable to help watch the other children, I set off to the only place a good mom and registered nurse takes her kids to be treated: Kroger.

Before I even left the driveway, I was a mess. It was midwinter in Ohio; the ground was covered in snow and the driveway in ice. The van doors were frozen shut, and in my attempt to shake them loose, I fell on the ice. Now with a sore rear-end, I corralled the kids through the front door of the van as I watched their snow boots leave mud all over my seat. At the clinic, the children made it their mission to make me look like the worst mom ever in front of the nurse practitioner: playing with the otoscope, asking for gloves, and opposing any instruction I gave them. Finally, we got a prescription, and headed to the pharmacy, where they gave us a twenty minute wait. Not too bad, unless of course you have four children with cabin fever inside a grocery store. At one point I lost Temperance, only to find her surrounded by a concerned crowd of adults, and once more, I am the worst mom ever. The final straw came back at the pharmacy twenty minutes later, when they claimed to have no recollection of my order, and proceeded to tell me that it will take another half hour to fill.

I lost it. I was no longer Mindy the unshakable; I had transformed into Mindy, the irritated, exhausted, and half-crazy. I left the store in utter frustration. Tears welled up as once more I watched my kids walk across my front seats with their muddy snow boots.

For me, it is not the big events that shake me up but the little things that build up throughout the day. What is it for you? Maybe it is when your plans are ruined. Maybe it is when people let you down. Maybe it is when the doctor has bad news, your marriage is on the rocks, or the bank account is drained.

Whatever it is that shakes you up, I want to encourage you to remember the disciples of Jesus and how they responded when they could have been shaken up and defeated.

They called the apostles in and had them flogged. Then they ordered them not to speak in the name of Jesus, and let them go. The apostles left the Sanhedrin, rejoicing because they had been counted worthy of suffering disgrace for the Name. Day after day, in the temple courts and from house to house, they never stopped teaching and proclaiming the good news that Jesus is the Messiah. —Acts 5:40–42

The religious leaders of their day had beaten and threatened them. I would call that a bad day. They were facing jail or death if they decided to continue preaching the gospel, and yet they left the council rejoicing! What? How can you rejoice when your life is on the line? How can you rejoice when your muscles are sore, your skin is burning, and your bones ache from beatings?

"They knew something we all need reminded of —that obstacles are an essential part of our story,"

These men were unshakable. They knew something we all need reminded of—that obstacles are an essential part of our story. Every obstacle we overcome makes us stronger. We serve an unshakable God, and your trials are no shock to Him. He is not intimidated by them, and you shouldn't be either.

Smile through Trial

So how do we become unshakable in such a volatile world? We need to learn to smile in the midst of trial. This is not natural, but in order to find strength in these tumultuous moments, we must force ourselves to do what is not natural. If you can learn to smile in the midst of trial, then over time, those little things won't get to you as much. That ditzy cashier will make you laugh, not yell. That inconsolable toddler won't steal your last nerve. That mountain of paperwork won't make you feel defeated, but motivated. That diagnosis will not be a threat to your life, but a challenge to overcome. You will begin to experience peace in chaos. You will find strength—like the disciples—that outlasts the threats and beatings. You will end your day rejoicing because you are unshakable.

Journal Prompts

Write down the things that have shaken you up lately. Talk to God about them, and allow His strength and unlimited power to give you peace amidst the chaos.

-4-
Broke Is No Joke

I know what it is to be in need, and I know what it is to have plenty. I have learned the secret of being content in any and every situation, whether well fed or hungry, whether living in plenty or in want. I can do all this through him who gives me strength.

—Philippians 4:12–13

"I can't believe I'm doing this. What kind of mother takes from her toddler's piggy bank to pay bills?" I thought as I emptied the few quarters and a couple dollar bills from my son's baby-blue porcelain pig.

The shame was heavy on me. I tried not to let him notice what Mommy was doing, but I had no choice. It was either do this or endure another overdraft fee from the bank. Lord knows they had given us enough grace on those in the past; they weren't going to let us slide again. So I counted up our change, made the deposit, and prayed that nothing else would hit the account before payday.

That's where we were in 2010—two little ones, a tiny house, and one old Cadillac with busted taillights, a torn ceiling, and no heat. Today, as I think back to those days, I can relate to the Apostle Paul in our scripture:

I know what it is to be in need, and I know what it is to have plenty. I have learned the secret of being content in any and every situation…

Is it possible to be content when you don't have enough money to pay the bills? Is it possible to be happy when the electric company is at the door—literally—and there's nothing you can do to stop them from shutting off your power? How can you have peace when you're so broke that you're stealing from your toddler?

I'm glad you asked. It was in that very season that Justin and I learned some critical lessons. We learned how to have faith to see the impossible. We learned to take God at His Word when there seemed to be no way. We learned to put Him first in our finances, even if we weren't sure how we were going to make it through the rest of the week. And, most importantly, we learned to be content in all circumstances.

"We found ways to make broke fun."

Gourmet Ramen

To this day, my son still enjoys a bowl of ramen noodles. Now he eats them because he thinks they're tasty. Back then, he ate them because that's all we could afford. He didn't know any different. He had no clue that it had been months since I'd bought anything from the meat department. He didn't notice how our cart compared to the others in the grocery store. He just knew that Mommy made some killer ramen noodles! We would call it "gourmet ramen." I would add eggs and cheese to make it more nutritious for him.

I remember being so jealous of people who could afford to get $200 worth of groceries, while I counted every item and prayed my card wouldn't be declined at the register. I remember that nervous feeling as I waited to see "approved" on the screen. I remember putting things back when I went over. I remember wishing I could get my children little prizes for good behavior, or even a Happy Meal with a toy in it. I remember buying their Christmas gifts secondhand online and adding in a few dollar-store finds. It was not an easy season for us, but... We found ways to make broke fun.

Third-World Mansion

As we all squished onto our purple hand-me-down couch to watch a movie, I looked over at Justin and said, "You know, one day, when we have a huge house and we're all in separate rooms, we're going to miss being squished onto one purple couch."

Our house was not anyone's dream, but we called it our "third-world mansion." We tried to keep things in perspective. Although we didn't have everything we wanted, we did have enough. We had a roof over our heads, a working vehicle, enough food for the day, and we had each other.

I figured there were people on the other side of the earth in third-world countries who would love to have our life. To them, our tiny house was a beautiful abode. So, as we dreamed about our future home with four bedrooms and a spacious backyard, we thanked God for our third-world mansion. Being content doesn't mean you can't dream about the future; it just means that you are grateful for what you already have as you look forward to a better future.

"Please pray for your cousin's baby to find a home."

The Day Everything Changed

Our finances didn't change overnight, but they certainly improved over the following years as we continued to trust God with what we had while waiting for the heavens to open—praying every day that He would open them sooner rather than later!

In 2011, God gave us an opportunity that would change our lives and our family forever, in every way. I received a text from my mom stating, "Please pray for your cousin's baby to find a home. The state is taking the baby away, and she will be in foster care unless someone steps up."

Even as I write this book, six and a half years later, tears well up in my eyes, thinking about the brevity of that moment. I forwarded the text on to my friends and began praying for this newborn baby girl to find a home. At that point, I was six months pregnant with our third child, Isabella, and making plans for her arrival. As I whispered "Amen" and looked up from my round belly, I heard the voice of the Father, saying, "This is her home." I looked around and saw a home that was prepared for a baby girl. "What is Justin going to say?" I thought. Later that day I tried to muster up the courage to tell him what I believed God was leading us to do. There was no easy or eloquent way to put it.

"I think we're supposed to take in this baby girl." I waited in the awkward silence for his response.

"For how long?" he said.

"I don't know. All I know is, I feel like God is saying that we are her home."

After a brief pause, and a deep breath, he said, "I trust you." And two weeks later, Temperance Donna Lynn was brought into our humble home.

Of course, there were so many things we didn't have time to figure out. How would we support another child when we were struggling so much already? What were we going to do about visits with her birth mom and dad? What if she had health challenges? What would we do when it was time to have Isabella and we had another infant at home? How would I care for two babies and two toddlers? What if we got attached and she was taken from us?

But none of that mattered. We could spend all day and night worrying about all the details, or we could walk by faith, and not by sight, trusting that if God had really asked us to do this, then He had a plan. And He certainly did.

"Our new life was a 180-degree difference from the year before. "

Within one year of that decision, we were living in a home three times bigger. We had turned in our old beat-up Cadillac for a family SUV, and we were given a minivan as a gift from a family member! Justin received a promotion at work, and I was making more as a nurse working overnights. Our new life was a 180-degree difference from the year before.

I believe that a huge reason for these blessings was our faithful obedience to God when it didn't make sense. We tithed when we didn't have enough to pay bills. We donated money to other broke people when we needed it ourselves, and we received an unexpected child into our home, without having any clue how we would care for her.

God is so good.

I recently looked back over some old journal entries. One of them had a description of my "dream home." I described a house with four bedrooms, a playroom for the kids, and a yard with plenty of sunshine. (Our previous backyard was covered by large oak trees, not allowing any sun through.)

Today, as I write this, I am sitting in our four-bedroom house, with a fully finished playroom big enough for twenty kids and a half-acre backyard with a little creek running through it, and lots and lots of sunshine!

"While you're on your way to your dream life, don't take your humble life for granted, but also never stop dreaming about what's possible when God is on your side!"

Write the Vision, Make It Plain

And the LORD answered me: "Write the vision; make it plain on tablets, so he may run who reads it."—Habakkuk 2:2 (ESV)

While you're on your way to your dream life, don't take your humble life for granted, but also never stop dreaming about what's possible when God is on your side! Write down your visions for the future. Don't be afraid to dream big, even when you have no clue how it could work out. Write down every detail of your dream home, dream family life, dream job, dream schedule, dream marriage. Write it down, and envision it often!

During that season when Justin and I were living in a tiny house with one old car, we would regularly take drives into beautiful neighborhoods and talk about what colors we would want on our home, what kind of stones would line the front of it, and what types of vehicles would fill our long driveway. And we haven't stopped dreaming big. Today, we dream about books we'll write, places we'll visit, adventures we'll go on, and what type of impact our children will make when they're our age.

We've never seen ourselves as broke people, even when we were. We never let our bank account, social status, pay grade, square footage, grocery budget, or crappy cars determine our identity. We were not, and have never been, defined by our "stuff." We are world changers, and nothing is going to stop us from changing the world—not even the electric guy!

So, friend, what's keeping you from feeling rich? An electric bill with big, bold red numbers on it? A grocery budget that will only allow for four days' worth of food? An entry-level job that barely covers childcare costs? A rickety old car? Hand-me-down clothes?

"Those things don't define you."

Those things don't define you. You are not poor. When you are rich in faith, you are rich, period. Next time you look in that mirror, you remind yourself who you are. You are a world-changer. You are an impact-maker. You have dreams and visions within you that can change everything. Enjoy those rags on your way to riches. They are a part of your story, and one day, you will be thankful for them. Until then, remember that you can do all things through Christ who gives you strength!

Scripture Study

Do not be anxious about anything, but in every situation, by prayer and petition, with thanksgiving, present your requests to God. – Philippians 4:6

Journal Prompts

What are you thankful for right now? Where do you see yourself in five years? If you could paint a picture of your ideal life, what would it look like? (Write the vision, make it plain.)

-5-

Flaws 'n' All

Now Peter and John were going up to the temple at the hour of prayer, the ninth hour. And a man lame from birth was being carried, whom they laid daily at the gate of the temple that is called the Beautiful Gate to ask alms of those entering the temple. Seeing Peter and John about to go into the temple, he asked to receive alms. And Peter directed his gaze at him, as did John, and said, "Look at us." And he fixed his attention on them, expecting to receive something from them. But Peter said, "I have no silver and gold, but what I do have I give to you. In the name of Jesus Christ of Nazareth, rise up and walk!" And he took him by the right hand and raised him up, and immediately his feet and ankles were made strong. And leaping up he stood and began to walk, and entered the temple with them, walking and leaping and praising God. And all the people saw him walking and praising God, and recognized him as the one who sat at the Beautiful Gate of the temple, asking for alms. And they were filled with wonder and amazement at what had happened to him.

— Acts 3:1–10 (ESV)

*T*he first full sermon I ever preached in a church was as copastor of Impact City. It was not perfect; it was far from incredible; and I have a hard time looking back and watching those first days of speaking, but...it was a step.

I imagine the first step that lame man took after Peter lifted him to his feet was a wobbly one. I bet he stumbled as he tried to learn the simple act of walking. I bet he looked a little silly at times, but he was walking in faith.

Since my first sermon, I have trained, studied, practiced, and polished my speaking skills, but to this day, when I step up to the stage, I am fully reliant on God. Even with my best effort, I need His grace. I know I cannot afford to go up there and speak on behalf of the King without the strength of the King. I'm still amazed when people come up and tell me how much my message helped them, or how it spoke directly to their heart, because usually I am already beating myself up internally, thinking of how I could have done better. I always say, "If it was good, it was God. If it was bad, it was me." God is calling you to do something you may have never thought possible. Within each of us are natural strengths, abilities, and talents, but also within each of us are weak areas in which God wants to shine. He wants to use us in those exact areas, to show the world His power, love, and glory. It is in these areas where we are weak that He is strong.

That is why, for Christ's sake, I delight in weaknesses, in insults, in hardships, in persecutions, in difficulties. For when I am weak, then I am strong. —2 Corinthians 12:10

I remember the first time I heard Lisa Bevere talk in person. She gave her story of being "dragged into speaking" by her husband. As she shared, her story resonated with me. I knew I'd felt a calling, not just to speak, but to bring hope, strength, comfort, and faith to those who were weak. I wanted to fulfill the calling God had placed on my life, but I knew how small and insignificant I was. I knew my weaknesses. I knew my lack of experience. I remembered speech class in high school—the pit I felt in my stomach every time I was asked to speak. I remembered dropping out of that class after just a couple weeks.

Even so, as Lisa spoke with such grace and confidence, her words touched my heart. I thought, if she can do it, maybe I can too. Then her husband John got up to speak, and he shared of his experience writing his first book. He admitted that English was not his favorite subject and writing was far from a strength of his. Yet, it was clear that God had asked him to write. John is now a best-selling author with books published in ninety languages!

"What is God asking you to do that seems impossible?"

What is God asking you to do that seems impossible? Whatever it is, know this: it will require more strength from God than you. Your own natural strengths will not do the trick. They may get you far, but not miracle-working, praiseworthy, glory-to-God far. In order to do the impossible, we have to be willing to allow God to use us in the very areas we have not shown ourselves to be strong in the past.

The crippled man at the gate had never walked since birth. He had sat at that gate day after day, begging for money. His weakness was physical. But one day, a man with no material offering gave him so much more than money. Peter didn't give him just the ability to walk, he gave him Jesus. Think about this: there were many people walking that day, many people using their legs to get through this gate called "Beautiful," but only one turned heads when he walked. Only one was rejoicing, praising, and giving God glory for his ability to walk. When he walked, everyone knew that it could only be by the power of God. When you step out into the unknown, believing that God can do the impossible through little ol' you, heads will turn. Even *you* will be amazed at what God does in your life when you allow Him to use your weakness for His glory.

Lessons from Kindergarten

Recently I was volunteering at a local elementary school. I was asked to sharpen pencils for a kindergarten classroom. As I was doing so, I noticed something interesting about all the pencils I was sharpening. The erasers had been used up on every one.

"I saw the hand of a child who didn't give up when they made a mistake."

Most people probably wouldn't have thought twice about this. Some people even walked by and mentioned how tedious a job I had been given. But I was grateful to have had this small, seemingly insignificant task of sharpening kindergarteners' pencils, because it inspired me. As I looked at each eraser that had been used down to the aluminum, I saw the hand of a child who didn't give up when they made a mistake. I saw little fingers that weren't quite strong enough yet to master the art of handwriting. I saw little minds that tried so hard to figure out simple addition but still got it wrong. I saw mark after mark that had to be erased and the tenacity of the young child who didn't give up.

Children are born with an incredible ability to keep trying even after so many failures. When did we learn to stop erasing? When did we decide that two or three mistakes were cause for quitting? Is it possible to get that childlike tenacity back? I have always been inspired and amazed by children—their outlook on life, their ability to laugh at everything, their amazement at the world around them, and their persistency. Every mother or father of a toddler has witnessed this persistency when their little one wanted ice cream after 8:00 p.m.

I have a theory. Maybe, just maybe, if we can learn how to erase and keep trying, like those kindergarteners, we can unlock new dreams, visions, and purposes within us.

Are you willing to erase your mistakes and try again? Are you willing to keep getting up after being knocked down? Are you willing to use that eraser all the way down to the aluminum? If so, dear friend, you will reach new heights. You will experience new things. You will soar on wings like eagles.

When you begin walking in faith, allowing God to use you, flaws and all, to do what you have never done, you may stumble. You might fall down. You may feel like everyone is watching you make a fool of yourself.

"One day, in that very area of your weakness, heads will turn and lives will be changed, miracles will happen, and people will know that it must have been God."

Don't stop walking. Don't stop being seen. Don't stop leaning on God's strength in your weakness, because one day, in that very area of your weakness, heads will turn and lives will be changed, miracles will happen, and people will know the it must have been God.

Scripture Study

But he said to me, "My grace is sufficient for you, for my power is made perfect in weakness." Therefore I will boast all the more gladly about my weaknesses, so that Christ's power may rest on me. That is why, for Christ's sake, I delight in weaknesses, in insults, in hardships, in persecutions, in difficulties. For when I am weak, then I am strong. – 2 Corinthians 12:9-10

Journal Prompts

Have you given up on a dream God placed in your heart? What purpose have you abandoned because of past failures? Which relationships are due for a spiritual erasing and fresh start? What areas of your life could use some childlike persistency?

-6-

When You're Overwhelmed

When we arrived in Macedonia, there was no rest for us. We faced conflict from every direction, with battles on the outside and fear on the inside.

—*2 Corinthians 7:5 (NLT)*

*D*o you have "the look"? You know, that one that says, "I'm exhausted. Don't talk to me unless you have cupcakes or a million dollars to hand me." Do you feel as if you are the only strong person you know? Do you feel like the world would simply fall apart if you took one day off from being you? I get it. I don't have enough appendages to count the times I've told Justin, "I'm just *overwhelmed.*"

I'm happy to tell you now that, although life is just as full as it's always been—and the pressure to have it all together and do it all is still there—I have found the cure for being overwhelmed. If you are anything like me, you are not going to want to hear this. It may seem counterintuitive, but the answer to this one is rest.

When your schedule is packed full and you are having

a hard time keeping up with the demands of life, you most likely have been running on adrenaline for far too long, not allowing enough time to rest and recharge. Research is proving the importance of rest and how a lack of rest affects our physical and mental health. When you go too long without rest, your body loses its strength to fight infections, and your mind begins to lose its ability to process things rationally. You may not be able to "feel" the good hormones diminishing and the stress hormones building, but what you do know is that if your toddler complains about the temperature of her food one more time, you are going to lose it. Or, if your boss sends you one more negative e-mail, you are walking out. Or, if that man of yours leaves his dirty boxers next to the hamper one more time, he's gonna find them, along with the rest of his stuff, in the front yard!

"These little things don't seem to bother us when we're rested and balanced, but when you live a restless, fast-paced life, they can quickly become the straw that breaks the camel's back."

These little things don't seem to bother us when we're rested and balanced, but when you live a restless, fast-paced life, they can quickly become the straw that breaks the camel's back. If this is you, you're probably trying to speed read this chapter to get to the "how-to" part and get on with your to-do list. (I know this because I have done it too.)

So here it is—it's time to regain control of your calendar, re-establish your balance, and make time for rest. If you don't have a calendar, get one. Then, schedule your priorities first. These include God time, marriage time, family time, and rest. If your calendar does not make time for these things, it's time to cut some things out and make room. Time is much like money. If you spend it God's way, He will make sure you have enough for everything else. If you try to fit in all the unimportant things first and then make time for God, family, and rest, you will never have time for them. You can tell yourself that you will read scripture and pray before bed, but after a long day of work, sports, homework, and whatever else you have on your plate, you may find that you can't even keep your eyes open, let alone read something or open your mouth to pray.

What does a balanced schedule look like? I make time for rest daily and weekly. Every day I rest for twenty minutes with zero distractions. I do this in the afternoon so that I can recharge for the rest of the day. Then, once a week, I schedule a couple hours of downtime into my calendar. This can be anything that helps you relax—taking a nap, watching your favorite show, reading, going to the salon, or taking a quiet walk. I also recommend to my busy mom friends to get away once a quarter to a place where you don't have to take care of anyone else.

You may be thinking, "Yeah, right. Sounds wonderful, but that's just not realistic in my life."

I get it. I've always been one to take on too many things and then find myself stuck in a schedule that I can't keep. I've always held more than one job, and I've never known adulthood without children. I can easily get to the place where

I feel like there is nothing I can do to change my crazy life.

"Nobody is going to come along and force you to take it easy."

But there is! You are in charge of your life. Nobody is going to come along and force you to take it easy. Nobody is going to take care of you. That's your job, and when you realize that it's a very important one, you'll find some things that need to change.

Help! I Don't Like People Anymore

I remember calling another pastor's wife one spring when I was overwhelmed and at my wit's end. I told her everything I was attempting to hold up and how it seemed like I was failing in everything. Then I got real honest and said, "And I don't like people anymore!"

I didn't know what was wrong with me, but it was like someone had stripped the empathy, kindness, and compassion right out of me. I didn't want to talk to people, pray for people, or hear about their problems. What good is a pastor who doesn't like people?

At that point she asked me, "What does your margin look

like?"

I said, "What's margin?"

She said, "You know. That time you spend on yourself, doing things you enjoy."

"Ha! You're serious? Um. There is none."

"Well, there's your problem. You can't help anyone else if you're not helping yourself."

So I began scheduling time for myself. Even if it was just to sit on the deck and enjoy the view, or—my favorite—take a drive through the country roads with worship music blasting and a fresh coffee in my hand. It was time for just me. And it was beautiful. It's amazing how quickly you can get refreshed. It doesn't take long before you're ready to go help someone else after resting with the Lord for a few minutes.

How did I do it? I had to say no to some things that seemed important. Was it hard? Absolutely. I like to make people happy. I like helping people. I like to save the day! So, when I decline invitations, or tell people I can't meet with them, it hurts. But I know that what my family and my church need most is for me to be healthy. So I put my time with God first, marriage and family time second, and then allowed for other things.

I also made the very difficult decision to enroll my kids in public school rather than homeschool them. Now, I am not saying that every kid should go to public school, or vice versa, but when I prayed about my schedule, it was obvious to me that homeschooling my son was not something I was graced to do. I had done it for almost two years, and for the last year, we'd fought every day. So after praying it over, I decided to enroll him in public school, beginning that next year. I thought I was failing him. I thought he would have a hard time transitioning. I thought he would struggle with the classroom structure, but man am I glad I made that decision!

"We pray every day that our kids will be followers of Jesus and leaders in their class, and it is happening!"

Today, all our kids are thriving in school, especially Kaden. He loves all the friends and activities and looks forward to going back after breaks. He has been placed in gifted classes and is loved by his peers. We pray every day that our kids will be followers of Jesus and leaders in their class, and it is happening! We hear story after story of how God is using our little ones to influence their peers in a positive way. God knew what was best for our family, but I wasn't seeing it until I prayed over my schedule and allowed Him to remove certain things from it.

Sabbath Rest

Every year Justin and I, along with our entire leadership team, seek God for one word that will define our focus for the year. This year, God gave Justin the word "Sabbath." He was hoping for "conquer" or "adventure" or something even more manly, but nope. God instructed Justin to make time to rest in Him this year.

That request seemed nearly impossible. Justin has worked

seven days a week since we planted the church. Of course we've taken vacations, and we schedule regular family nights and date nights, but he hasn't had a scheduled day of rest for as long as he can remember. This is the illustration that the Holy Spirit gave Justin: it's like golfing. You have to let the club do the work. When it comes to life—and golf—Justin has always been a "grip it and rip it" kind of guy. If you work hard enough, long enough, you will succeed.

"There are some things in life that you can't fix by working harder."

That works for a while, but at some point, you come to the realization that you can't be everything to everyone and there are some things in life that you can't fix by working harder. Just like sometimes you can put all your strength and energy into whacking that little white ball and end up in the woods.

So this year, Justin has begun letting the club do the work, God being the club. This doesn't mean we do nothing. Of course, there has to be a hand and an arm to swing, but there is a God element that we cannot ignore. We can't do God's part, and God won't do our part. The key to this is remembering that we aren't going to succeed at life in our own strength.

One way to show God that you trust in Him is to obey the Sabbath and rest. When we do less, God can do more.

"He won't give you peace over something He hasn't called you to."

Bless These Cupcakes

You cannot afford to keep living an overbooked, over-stretched lifestyle and expect peace and happiness. That's about as foolish as I am when praying for God to bless my dinner of cupcakes and Doritos. God is not going to remove the calories from my cupcakes, and He won't give you peace over something He hasn't called you to. So, if you feel like you're rushing through life, stretching yourself too thin and doing a million things you weren't called to do, and you're waiting for God to somehow wash over you with peace, don't be surprised when it doesn't come. Sometimes the tension we feel is a call to make a change.

I'll never forget the line I heard from a pastor and mentor of ours: "Everyone knows you can't do everything, but they all still want you to do their thing." It's easy to find yourself burning the candle at both ends, but that life isn't helpful for anyone. You have to know the difference between what is important and what simply appears urgent.

There are few real emergencies in life. Will that friend survive if you don't take her eighth call for the day? Probably. Will your family member forgive you for missing her fourth party of the month? Probably. Will your workplace make it without you if you take a personal day every now and then? Probably.

Now I'm not saying that you should never help people. There is much fruit in the labor of helping people. I am saying that if you find yourself saying, "I don't like people anymore!" it may be time to take care of yourself.

Scripture Study

By the seventh day God had finished the work He had been doing; so on the seventh day He rested from all His work. — Genesis 2:2

Come to me, all you who are weary and burdened, and I will give you rest. – Matthew 11:28

Journal Prompts

Make a list of your responsibilities. Then decide which ones only you can do, which ones you must do, and which ones you enjoy doing. Pray for God to guide your schedule. Then plan your next time of rest.

-7-
Get Off the Guilt-Trip

Therefore, there is now no condemnation for those who are in Christ Jesus.

—*Romans 8:1*

What's your most embarrassing moment—that moment in time that you wish with every fiber of your being that you could go back and change? For me, there are many! I've ran my face into screen doors in front of an entire table of in-laws. I've done the "flying squirrel" onto a concrete slab when Justin dodged my leap for a piggy-back ride. Our congregation will never let me forget the time I made a minor mistake in verbiage and announced that we were proud to partner with the City of Pataskala and our local "Lion's Den" (an area adult bookstore) to offer the annual "Light the Night" fireworks show! Yep. That would make for fireworks, but probably not the ones we were expecting.

The most recent was at our "Night to Remember" event

for couples at our church. Surrounded by eighty of our church members, Justin and I attempted the *Dirty Dancing* lift. You know the one. The epic stunt that even Patrick Swayze had a hard time nailing. Our success rate on this particular stunt was about 5 percent, but we went for it anyway, not considering the wardrobe factor. I was wearing a slim black dress. This happened to be the only time in history that I did not supplement my ensemble with hose or leggings. I ran. I jumped. He lifted. And as he lifted, up went my dress. Midair I thought, "This is about to become my most mortifying moment in life." I clung to the bottom of my dress with all the strength within me, and as a result, fell straight to the ground. Epic. Fail.

Is there a feeling worse than embarrassment? In the moment, it certainly doesn't seem like it. Shortly after, we feel defined and labeled by our mistake. We make attempts to laugh it off, cover it up, make an excuse, or pin the blame on someone else to get rid of that awful feeling. But there is a level of embarrassment that becomes much more than a passing feeling. It's the feeling you have when you've done something that was not only embarrassing, but wrong. Something that clings to you, forms your identity, and weighs you down. That feeling is guilt.

"Somewhere underneath the skimpy outfit, makeup, and high heels, there was a girl who loved God."

Mirror, Mirror

There is nothing more paralyzing than guilt—and I too have had my fair share of it. I can still remember like yesterday looking into the bathroom mirror in the basement of a bar. I had had so much to drink that I stumbled as I made my way to the sink. And when I looked up, it was as if I was looking at someone else. Deep down, somewhere underneath the skimpy outfit, makeup, and high heels, there was a girl who loved God—who was called to a great purpose—but in the mirror stood a lost, dizzy, drunk girl. I remember feeling so ashamed of myself that I couldn't look any longer. I was like a dog who wouldn't look at the shoe he had chewed up.

It wasn't just one night. There were countless nights I found myself avoiding the mirror at 2:00 a.m., hoping that if I didn't look, I wouldn't have to face the guilt and shame that accompanied it. There were countless mornings I woke up feeling so guilty for the stupid things I'd said, the stupid things I'd done for attention, and the mistakes that would have lasting consequences. I kept going to church because I knew I needed it, but I arrived more and more hungover from the nights before.

"Only God, in all His grace and mercy, could see all that I had done and say, " I have grace for that."

Thinking back to that season, I am overwhelmed with gratitude to a God who somehow looked at that mess of a girl and called her chosen. Only God, in all His grace and mercy, could see all that I had done and say, "I have grace for that."

At age twenty-one, pregnant with our first son, I lifted my guilty hands to God and prayed that He would give me a second chance at following Him. I recommitted my life to Christ and received His unfailing love and unlimited forgiveness for my every sin. I got baptized for the second time, in a hotel swimming pool.

Then, Justin and I began taking steps toward a new life—one that wasn't our way, but His way. We made a commitment to abstain from alcohol for one year. We removed ourselves from the bar scene and made some new friends at church. We started serving God together, volunteering in any way they would let us. We came alive! We found purpose! We experienced a new freedom that wasn't wild and irresponsible. This freedom came from knowing we were loved, accepted, and forgiven.

It's been over ten years since that night I stumbled into that dirty bar bathroom, but I can still remember that awful feeling of shame and guilt. Maybe you know what that feels like. Maybe you still struggle with it. Maybe you have a hard time believing that God really wants to forgive you for everything—the little stuff and the big stuff. Maybe there are people in your life who haven't forgotten and still hold that guilt over your head like a dark cloud.

You don't have to live that way. You can find strength through the freedom that comes from forgiveness today. Hand your burdens, mistakes, failures, and past over to the only One big enough to handle it. Ask God to take that weight off your shoulders. Ask Him to wash you clean from all that guilt and shame. The Bible says that if we will confess our sins, He is faithful and just to forgive them.

He has removed our sins as far from us as the east is from the west. —Psalm 103:12 (NLT)

Growth Killer

Life is hard enough without the weight of guilt. Paying bills, managing schedules, cleaning the house, parenting children—it's all hard! And one way the enemy adds insult to injury is to tempt us to feel guilty for what we are going through. For instance, if the bank account is low and you are having a hard time making rent, you may start to feel bad for not picking up that overtime. When you're busy and there's not enough time in the day to get everything accomplished, but you're so exhausted that you choose a moment of rest over productivity, the enemy may try to make you feel guilty for taking care of yourself. That is a small example, but it can be much worse. Maybe you lost a loved one, and on top of the pain and grief you are already dealing with, you are experiencing guilt for not having spent more time with him or her.

"Guilt has a way of paralyzing our growth and killing our purpose."

Guilt has a way of paralyzing our growth and killing our purpose. Even as I write today, I fight off feelings of guilt for not finishing this book sooner, for not making more time to write in the past few weeks. If I allowed those feelings to continue, they could make me feel so bad that I'd lose my motivation to do anything.

Have you been there before? Have you felt so bad for not doing enough that you decided to not do anything at all? This can happen in any area of life, from marriage to our day jobs, and even things as simple as housework. We may start to feel behind, and the enemy brings to mind more and more areas of life that we are deficient in, making us feel like a failure in every area, and before you know it, we are convinced that we are a worthless excuse for a human being. This is how great people with great purpose in life get to the point of quitting on everything. Listen, friend, we cannot afford to listen to these lies.

The truth is, there is no condemnation in Christ Jesus. God is not putting guilt on you for what you have or have not done; in fact, Jesus came to free us up from that guilt. Galatians 5:1 states, "For freedom Christ has set us free; stand firm therefore, and do not submit again to a yoke of slavery." This means there *will be* opportunities to submit ourselves to the bondage of guilt or shame, but we must resist those temptations and remind ourselves that if God does not condemn us, then we cannot let any man, including ourselves, condemn us either.

"When we carry guilt for our past sins, it's as if we're telling Jesus, "Your death wasn't enough for me."

What is it lately that has caused you to feel guilt, shame, or condemnation? Decide today that you will not accept those feelings but rather accept the freedom that you have in Christ! God sent His Son to die for those sins. There is no mistake you have made that is too great for the cross to cover. When we carry guilt for our past sins, it's as if we're telling Jesus, "Your death wasn't enough for me." You wouldn't dare say that to Jesus, so don't you dare hold onto that guilt any longer. It's not yours to carry. And when people try to give it back to you, refuse. When the enemy gets in your head and tries to remind you of your sins, you fight back. You remind him that he has been defeated along with your sin! He has no power over you unless you allow it. And your sin has no weight on you unless you allow it. Don't go another day walking in shame and guilt. Draw a line in the sand; mark it on your calendar. Today is your freedom day!

Scripture Study

It is for freedom that Christ has set us free. Stand firm, then, and do not let yourselves be burdened again by a yoke of slavery. – Galatians 5:1

Therefore, there is now no condemnation for those who are in Christ Jesus. – Romans 8:1

Journal Prompts

What has been weighing you down lately? What past mistakes still make you feel ashamed? What does the cross mean to you? What does freedom mean to you?

-8-

When You're Only Lonely

Then the LORD God said, "It is not good that the man should be <u>alone</u>; I will make him a helper suitable for him."

—Genesis 2:18 [emphasis mine]

*E*ven in paradise, when everything was perfect, it was still not good for man to be alone. We are meant for relationships, with God and with others, but relationships can be messy. People can be tough. People test your patience. They can do and say things that hurt. They have the ability to put you in a bad mood with one smart comment, one Facebook post, one action (or lack of action), one text message, and sometimes just a look! And yet, none of us want to go through life alone, so we pray for God to give us a husband, a wife, a best friend, good coworkers. We pray for God to bless us with children. Then, years later, we're complaining to God about the very people we prayed for!

"God, if you don't fix this man…"

"God, I can't handle this child!"

"Lord, why would my friend say such hurtful things?"

"Lord, I can't work with these people!"

Relationships are hard. People are difficult. But worst of all, they hurt. Chances are, whether you are fifteen or seventy-five, you have experienced some sort of relational pain. Someone, at some point, said something that cut you to the core. Someone you trusted betrayed you. Someone you respected lost all your respect. Someone you confided in gossiped behind your back. We've all been there, and the trouble with relational pain is that it causes us to isolate.

Our hurt feelings, anger, resentment, and grieving remind us of the risk we took in allowing people to get close. We think:

"I knew he didn't really love me."

"I knew she couldn't be trusted."

"I should never have poured my heart out to her."

And, in our pain, we make a decision: "I will never let this happen again."

But the only way to avoid relational pain is to avoid relationships. So we isolate. Maybe we even stay married, keep our job, or keep going out with friends, but we never allow anyone to get close enough to hurt us again. We build walls around our heart. Walls around our weaknesses. Walls around our true self. Walls that keep relationships at a safe distance, and us in a lonely, dark place.

"Isolation makes us vulnerable to the enemy."

If you find yourself in that place, listen up, friend, because this may be the entire reason you picked up this book. Isolation makes us vulnerable to the enemy. There is no more dangerous place to be when you are in pain than in isolation. I have learned that one of the enemy's greatest tactics is to use relational pain to cause isolation, so he can succeed in accomplishing his next act of destruction in our lives.

Be alert and of sober mind. Your enemy the devil prowls around like a roaring lion looking for someone to devour. —1 Peter 5:8

When you allow relational pain to isolate you from the relationships you were meant to be in, you make yourself an easy target for the enemy.

I'll admit that I have a tendency to go through periods of isolation. I can be surrounded by people—thousands of Facebook friends, four children tugging my leg, an incredible family just a phone call away, and hundreds of church members supporting me—and still feel lonely at times.

It wasn't long ago I found myself in a church parking lot crying crocodile tears because of all the pressure to be and do everything for everyone. I felt as if I was failing in every area of life, but worst of all, I felt as if there was no one who understood. I had allowed pressure to become self-pity, which spiraled into an emotional mess in some random church parking lot. I felt like there was nobody I could call that would understand. There was nobody in the world who was attempting to do what I was attempting to do. I was all alone in my misery. On top of all the pressure, the feeling of loneliness made it worse.

"If the enemy can get you alone, he's already won the first battle."

But as I sat there praying, I realized what had happened. I had lost battle number one. You see, if the enemy can get you alone, he's already won the first battle. So I picked up the phone and reluctantly called the first woman who came to mind. In that simple phone call, I won the next battle against the enemy, by surrounding myself with another believer who could join me in prayer.

The Word says, "For where two or three are gathered together in my name, there am I in the midst of them." —Matthew 18:20 (KJV)

God has created us for relationships, with Him and with others! Most believers don't have any trouble realizing their need for a relationship with God, but there is too large a portion of believers who are under the impression that they don't need a church, small groups, accountability partners, or anything else that involves people.

The Bible disagrees with this thought process. From the beginning of time God proclaimed that it was not good for man to be alone, and His mind hasn't changed. Take a look at Ecclesiastes 4:9–12:

> *Two are better than one, because they have a good return for their labor: If either of them falls down, one can help the other up. But pity anyone who falls and has no one to help them up. Also, if two lie down together, they will keep warm. But how can one keep warm alone? Though one may be overpowered, two can defend themselves. A cord of three strands is not quickly broken.*

We were made for three-strand relationships—relationships with people and God that are not easily broken when they get messy, difficult, or painful. A marriage with Christ at the center will not break. A family with Christ woven within it will not break. A friendship based on the Word of God, and not the word of the latest *Cosmopolitan* magazine, will not break. When we allow relational pain to isolate us, we not only become vulnerable to the enemy, but when we're down, there is no one there to lift us up.

What kind of world would this be if everyone decided they didn't need anyone else?

"We must get away to be with God, but not forget our place amongst the crowd."

I should give you this disclaimer: not all alone time is bad. We need people in our lives, but there is a place for alone time. Our bodies, souls, and spirits require a specific amount of alone time in order to find refreshment, renewal, peace, prayer, and union with God. For some who are more introverted (like myself), we need more alone time than our social counterparts. Regardless of your personality, alone time is necessary to us being our best, and Jesus was the best example. He would regularly get away and devote stretches of time to prayer before heading back to the crowds that were eager to see him. So, in following His example, we must get away to be with God, but not forget our place amongst the crowd, which is what we'll cover next.

Embrace Your Place

I heard a life-changing message from the incredible Christine Cain about "embracing your place." She mentioned this scripture:

> *For as in one body we have many members, and the members do not all have the same function, so we, though many, are one body in Christ, and individually members one of another. Having gifts that differ according to the grace given to us, let us use them. —Romans 12:4–6 (ESV)*

Christine went on to encourage us all to take our place in

the kingdom of God, amongst His people, to fulfill the purpose God has for each of us. There is a great suffering amongst the body of Christ when it is missing members.

Even positions as small and seemingly insignificant as a pinky toe have a great purpose in the body, and when they are not in place, the body suffers.

Let me explain. It was about fifteen years ago. Justin and I were on spring break from college, vacationing in none other than Panama City Beach. Some may call it the party capital of spring break. We now call it the portal to hell—not because of the story I am about to share, but many other stories that won't make it into this book. This was our "B.C. life," as we say—before we surrendered our lives to Jesus.

We were partaking in spring break festivities and enjoying the sun when we heard of an oceanside competition. Each couple was given an extra-large T-shirt to fit in together and challenged to a sandy race to the finish line. We gave it our very best, and the good news is, we won! Yay for free T-shirts!

The bad news is, somewhere along the race, my pinky toe met with Justin's steel heel and fractured. A tiny little pinky toe being out of place may not seem like a big deal, but I had been preparing to try out for The Ohio State University Cheer Team two weeks later. I had put years of my life and thousands of dollars into training for this moment, to become an OSU cheerleader, but when the time came to land that standing back-tuck, the pain of that fractured pinky toe affected my whole body, and I fell flat on my face. The coaches said I would have made the team if I could have landed that skill. Lesson learned: don't race on the beach for a T-shirt, and pinky toes *do* matter.

"You have been given a position in the body of Christ to fulfill a mission in the body of Christ."

Maybe today you don't feel like much. You may not see any value in your work, your home life, your place at church, your family, or even your marriage. Maybe you have been tempted lately to retreat to isolation: to stop going to church, to quit trying so hard at work, to step down from volunteering. Don't allow your "small part" make you feel insignificant. You are important. You have purpose. You have skills, talents, gifts, abilities, and passions that other people don't have. Without you, the body would suffer. Without you, someone will hurt.

You have been given a position in the body of Christ to fulfill a mission in the body of Christ. Take your position, as small or large as it may be, and never allow the enemy to convince you it's not important.

Jesus was humble enough to take the position of Emmanuel (God with us) in order to fulfill the mission of becoming our Savior. I cannot imagine the discomfort He felt as He left heaven, to become man in the most humble form. I can't imagine the strength it took to subject Himself to ridicule, beatings, betrayal, and ultimately crucifixion, all undeserved. He went first. He endured the pain of relationships to take His position as our Savior, knowing without Him, we could never be saved, and He asks you and I to take our position amongst imperfect, hypocritical, and undeserving people to fulfill our missions. It may not always be ideal, but it will definitely be worth it in the end to hear Him say, "Well done, good and faithful servant."

Scripture Study

Be joyful in hope, patient in affliction, faithful in prayer. Share with the Lord's people who are in need. Practice hospitality. Bless those who persecute you; bless and do not curse. Rejoice with those who rejoice; mourn with those who mourn. Live in harmony with one another. Do not be proud, but be willing to associate with people of low position. – Romans 12:12-16

Journal Prompts

Jesus took the humble position of a human baby in a manger in order to fulfill the mission of becoming your Savior. What does that mean for your life? What position have you been given in your workplace, family, and church? How can you embrace that place?

Are there walls up over your heart, protecting you from relational pain but ultimately preventing you from living the life God has for you? What is one step you can take to bring those walls down?

-9-

Strength to Fight

For our struggle is not against flesh and blood, but against the rulers, against the authorities, against the powers of this dark world and against the spiritual forces of evil in the heavenly realms.

—*Ephesians 6:12*

*E*very once in a while we experience the perfect storm: a culmination of emotions, ideas, passions, and trial that propels us into the next season. Oftentimes, these storms come in undesirable forms.

It was after an incredible victory in our church and our small group that I received one of those texts that just sets you back and consumes your mind. That text, along with the mountains of mess to clean, monumental meetings on the schedule, financial pressure, and my own personal shame for not being further along in this darn book, had brought me to precipice of conviction and spurred on some overdue decisions that needed to be addressed.

Before spewing my unpolished emotions onto anyone, I asked the necessary questions:

"Self, are you PMSing? No. Okay, good. I hate when that happens. Self, are you exhausted? No, I got a good seven hours of sleep and my essential power nap today. Then it's settled. This is a legit and necessary issue that needs addressed. Let's find a human with ears. Ah, there he is. My counselor, voice of reason, partner in life, and daily brawling buddy, Justin."

As it were, Justin was not in the same mental state as I was, as he hadn't been down the mental, emotional, and spiritual journey I had taken in the last five minutes, but that didn't stop me from pursuing it.

"Let's go talk alone in the bedroom," I said as I walked off.

But all he heard was, "Let's talk."

Hence, I sat in the bedroom and he sat at the kitchen table, both of us naively assuming the other was coming any minute…for ten minutes. Finally, I stomped back downstairs to find him confused and frustrated.

"Do you realize you asked me to talk and then walked away for ten minutes?" he said.

Thus began World War III.

"My spouse is not my enemy."

After a good screaming match about nothing important, we parted ways to cool down. I picked up the closest journal I could find and finally did what I should have done to begin with: speak to God about my emotions, passions, convictions, and desires.

Justin and I are very good fighters. We can fight about nearly anything. If you ever need advice on how to make a mountain out of a molehill in your marriage, let's talk because I have a lot of experience! We're both very passionate, driven, tenacious people with voices that desire to be heard. This can be dangerous when it comes to conflict, but it also can be healthy, because we won't allow anything to go unaddressed. We confront and resolve every issue that rears its ugly head at us, and usually it's beaten and behind us before the end of the day.

The issue arises when we fail to remember one very important principle:

My spouse is not my enemy.

That evening, there was a real, unseen enemy that was in full force against my family, my marriage, my purpose, and my peace. Once I got alone and spoke to God, I was able to see clearly what I needed to do and believe in God for His miraculous power to do the rest. As I felt tears wanting to well up in my eyes, I pulled them back, put on my fighter face, and charged hell with all I had. I prayed a fervent prayer for my extended family who was under attack; I petitioned heaven for answers, peace, healings, restoration, and new purpose; and I put the enemy back in his place. I wrote down the desires of my heart and believed God for all of it. I wrote until my hand was shaking and all of the righteous anger in me had been poured out onto the pages.

"Sometimes it takes a storm to blow us into a new place."

Afterward, I found Justin in a similar position, praying and worshipping God, and the two of us were able to have a faith-filled conversation and make some decisions that would change the course of our year.

Sometimes it takes a storm to blow us into a new place. Sometimes it takes pressure from all angles to make us angry enough, fed up enough, ready enough to do something about it. In those times, we have to remember who our enemy is. We must not forget that it is okay to be angry, but our anger should be focused in the right direction.

> *Be angry, and do not sin: do not let the sun go down on your wrath. —Ephesians 4:26 (NKJV)*

When we get angry at our spouse, our family, our boss, or our kids, we are missing it. That anger doesn't do a bit of good. But, when we direct our anger toward the true enemy of our souls, we can fight the good fight against the powers of darkness, and good will come from it.

"Be encouraged friend—if you are under attack, then you must be a force to be reckoned with."

That night, I was able to muster up the courage to face the true unseen enemy and fight a good fight. I was able to channel those emotions into tenacity and productivity and make some changes that would expand God's kingdom and bring Him glory.

I don't know what kind of storm you're facing. I don't know who has been angering you. I don't know what kind of pressure you are under. But I know this: there is an enemy out there, whose goal is to steal, kill, and destroy you. He wants to destroy your marriage, your family, your purpose, and your joy. Those people who anger you are not your enemy, and it will do no good to fight them. Be encouraged friend— if you are under attack, then you must be a force to be reckoned with. So draw your spiritual sword, the Word of God; put the power of prayer to work; and fight the good fight of faith.

Turn your tears into tenacity and make the enemy tremble for ever daring to torture you.

Scripture Study

Fight the good fight of the faith. Take hold of the eternal life to which you were called when you made your good confession in the presence of many witnesses. —1 Timothy 6:12

And we know that God causes everything to work together for the good of those who love God and are called according to His purpose for them. —Romans 8:28 (NLT)

Journal Prompts

What or who have you allowed to anger you lately? What can you do in this storm to put your faith in God? Are there desires in your heart that God is calling you to address?

-10-

Strength to Keep Going

Let us not become weary in doing good, for at the proper time we will reap a harvest if we do not give up.

—*Galatians 6:9*

*H*ave you been tempted to lose heart lately? Does it seem like things are never going to change? Do you look around at your life and feel sorry for yourself? Don't allow that toxic thinking to root too deeply in your mind, because it will destroy your future! Be encouraged, friend—your time is coming.

Overlooked and Underwhelmed

Before Impact City was a twinkle in our eye, before we were pastors, and before anyone knew the calling on our life, there lived a frustrated young woman who had been on her knees desperately praying for God to use her. I knew without a shadow of a doubt that God had called me into ministry, yet

I found myself overlooked and underwhelmed.

When I was sixteen, I heard God for the first time. That still, small voice whispered that I would be a part of something great for Him. I called my dad and told him immediately. I knew this was the voice of God, because I had never experienced anything like it before. But years later, after changing my life, and serving in the church as much as possible, I felt as if my time would never come. There were passions stirring within me that needed an outlet! I had so much to give, and so much to say to those who were hurting, but it seemed as if every door was closed. Doors opened for other people, and even for Justin. He was invited to teach a sermon at our home church, and offered a staff position. At the time of the job offer, it was made clear to us that, if he accepted, I would be the "invisible employee". This meant, I would be helping Justin from home, but never really seen or heard. I can remember being so frustrated that I wanted to scream. Why would God put a desire in my heart and then let it die? What was I doing wrong? Why wouldn't anyone give me a chance?

I did everything I knew to do to make things work in my timing. I offered to sing on the worship team. They weren't interested. I offered to help with announcements. They weren't interested. I offered to make care calls and pray with anyone who needed encouragement. They weren't interested. I even went to the extent of applying for an entry-level job at a Christian radio station. Even if I had to scrub their toilets, I would be okay knowing I was working in the ministry.

What I didn't know then, was that I was living out God's perfect timing. He knew what He had for me. He knew that one day, sooner than expected, He would give me more opportunity than I could handle. My dream was just around the corner, if I would just keep going.

Taking Jesus to Prison

Since I wasn't able to minister publicly, I began using my ministry gifts at home. I started by recording short devotional videos while the kids were napping. I would post these little videos titled "encouragement", in hopes of helping at least one person that needed hope. Some days I would reach five people, some days I felt like they didn't help anyone. But I didn't stop, even after being told that I wasn't supposed to do that type of thing. Those silly little videos have since turned into a wonderful online ministry.

Another unexpected turn led me to an unlikely place – prison. One day I decided to tag along with an older woman from our church as she ministered to the youth in a nearby juvenile correctional facility. She taught me how to talk to inmates and share the gospel. I would drive an hour across town to pour lemonade for inmates and pray with them after she preached.

One day she couldn't make it. She asked me to share the message. I was nervous, and I didn't know what to say, but she believed God would give me a word. I walked into that prison full of guys, and preached with all the passion and energy I had. As I was speaking, it was like a river dam was opened for the first time. In that moment, God's word began to flow out of me like living water and scriptures I didn't realize I knew flew off my tongue. To my surprise, at the close of my sermon, dozens of hands went up across the room, receiving salvation. Lesson learned: when you are faithful with little things, like pouring lemonade, God will trust you with bigger things, like bringing His people to salvation.

Those early steps on this ministry path were a bit wobbly, but I kept stepping. I learned to humble myself and serve people, regardless of who got the credit. I learned to love people, understand people, and encourage people from all walks of life. I ministered to homeless men on the street, tired moms in small group, and random people I met just living life. More opportunities came. After a while of ministering in any outlet God would provide, Justin and I were offered jobs at several churches across the country. This time, we would be hired as a team. The offers were all great, and it was hard to know which was right, so we prayed. It was then that God told Justin to turn down all the jobs, and plant a church right here in our town.

What?! Plant a church? We don't know the first thing about church planting. We're not supposed to be the top guys yet. We still have learning to do! But God doesn't change his mind when you give him all your excuses. He knew who He was calling, and He knew it was time.

So just like that, we began the process of training, planning, and gathering people. We began with sixteen of our closest friends and family. A year later, on February 16, 2014, we became Impact City Church.

Today, I no longer feel overlooked and underwhelmed. Today, I am overwhelmed with opportunity to minister to God's people. I am living my dream, and it is such an adventure. Looking back, I wouldn't change my path for anyone else's. I cherish those memories of the first low-quality encouragement videos I made in my kitchen, and the special moments I had with those inmates.

Get Out from Under the Broom Tree!

Elijah was afraid and ran for his life. When he came to Beer-sheba in Judah, he left his servant there, while he himself went a day's journey into the wilderness. He came to a broom bush, sat down under it and prayed that he might die. "I have had enough, Lord," he said. "Take my life; I am no better than my ancestors." Then he lay down under the bush and fell asleep. —1 Kings 19:3–5

"Have you ever been so tired, so spent, so stressed, so burnt out that you just want to quit on life, or at least make time stop for a while?"

Elijah was the mighty prophet of the Lord—the man who performed miracles, made fire rain down from heaven, and stopped the rain—and there he was, hiding under a bush, begging the Lord to take his life.

Have you ever been in a similar place? Have you ever been so tired, so spent, so stressed, so burnt out that you just want to quit on life, or at least make time stop for a while?

Maybe you are exhausted from parenting little ones, and you just want one day to rest. Maybe you have been working overtime to provide for your family, and you're wondering if the toll on your body is worth it. Maybe you have been taking care of a sick loved one, and you find yourself resenting them and their sickness because of what it has taken from you. Maybe you just feel like quitting. That's how Elijah, an incredible man of God, felt in this moment in scripture. He was so spent that he wanted to die. I can relate. I'm gonna get real honest with you. I remember being so tired and overwhelmed that I dreamt of being hospitalized: "If I just step out in front of this car," I thought, "they'll have to put me in the hospital and I won't have to keep up this messy house, make dinner, or rock a screaming child for at least a couple days." Maybe I am the only mom who has ever had that ridiculous thought, or maybe I just helped you feel understood. Either way, it's sadly true.

It was in the season when I was raising two babies and two toddlers. The days were long and exhausting. I wasn't completely a stay-at-home mom but a working-part-time mom, while attempting to be with the kids as much as possible to avoid paying a sitter. I felt the demands of keeping up with the home, the kids' schedules, our marriage, church roles, all while attempting to make a few bucks as a nurse to help with the budget. I can remember feeling like I would be raising babies for forever and eternity, like those little guys were never going to learn how to make their own sandwich!

Those days, I counted down the hours until I knew relief was coming. I was like a kid on the way to Disney World: "Are we there yet?" or more accurately, "Is he home yet?" I remember going all day without slowing down, all day without a break. I remember eating my meals with one hand while the baby attempted to swat every bite out of my other one. And Justin would get home…skipping through the door like Cinderella, with a big ole smile on his face like he had just gotten back from Disney World. And he'd ask, "Hey, honey, what have you guys been up to all day?"

And I would respond, with a glare on my face, "I…don't… know! I cannot tell you one thing that I have managed to accomplish today, but I can tell you ten things I haven't done! I haven't showered, I haven't finished a meal, I haven't put my feet up. I haven't stepped foot out of the house, I haven't spoken with an adult…Should I go on?!"

And I can remember being so envious of him because he got to drive all by himself to and from work. While I was wiping baby puke off my shirt for the tenth time, he was having company lunch breaks and frolicking through the office without tiny human attachments.

But like I said, friends, your time is coming.

Now, all four of our kids are in school. And today…while he's sitting through another meeting, I'm contemplating whether I want to take my afternoon nap now or sit on the deck and watch the clouds roll by.

Do not grow weary. Life is hard. Schedules are busy, but if you are keeping your priorities straight and doing what the Lord is asking you to do, you can ensure that there is a season of rest in your future.

All at once an angel touched him and said, "Get up and eat."
He looked around, and there by his head was some bread baked over hot coals, and a jar of water. He ate and drank and then lay down again. The angel of the LORD came back a second time and touched him and said, "Get up and eat, for the journey is too much for you." So he got up and ate and drank. Strengthened by that food, he traveled forty days and forty nights until he reached Horeb, the mountain of God. —1 Kings 19:5–8

"But Elijah would have never found Elisha if he had stayed under that broom tree."

God had a plan for Elijah—a plan to send him to a young man who would become a disciple and a partner, and who would eventually accept a double portion of Elijah's anointing. But Elijah would have never found Elisha if he had stayed under that broom tree. His new partner, Elisha, went on to perform more recorded miracles than anyone except Jesus. What if Elijah had given up? What if he had allowed the threats, stress, and fatigue to stop him for good?

Friend, it's time to get out from under that broom tree, eat some food, and get on with your calling. Your time is coming. Rest is coming. Help is on the way. God has a partner prepared for you that will encourage you, and bring you support when you're weary. A new season of fruitfulness and joy is coming, but it won't find you under that tree. Get up, get out, and don't stop moving until the Lord says so!

Scripture Study

David was greatly distressed because the men were talking of stoning him; each one was bitter in spirit because of his sons and daughters. But David found strength in the LORD his God. —1 Samuel 30:6

Let us not become weary in doing good, for at the proper time we will reap a harvest if we do not give up. – Galatians 6:9

Journal Prompts

Share your honest thoughts with the Lord. Tell Him how you're feeling and what is causing you frustration. Ask for help, both spiritually and physically. Thank God for a time in your life when He came through. Write down your hopes and desires for the future.

-11-

Moving Past Our Past

Brothers and sisters, I do not consider myself yet to have taken hold of it. But one thing I do:
Forgetting what is behind and straining toward what is ahead, I press on toward the goal to win the prize for which God has called me heavenward in Christ Jesus.
—Philippians 3:13–14

One thing pastoring people has taught me is that we all have a reason for being messed up, and usually it stems from a past relationship. We can all connect our current shortcomings with some bad relationship (or lack of relationship) in our past:

"My parents never took me to church, so I have a hard time believing in God."

"My parents took me to church every Sunday, so I associate church with punishment."

"My parents forced me to memorize scripture when I was bad, so I don't like the Bible."

"My parents never taught me anything about the Bible, so I feel behind in my faith."

"My parents never showed me affection, so I don't know how to be affectionate."

"My parents sheltered me from the world, so I'm not comfortable in it."

"My dad was never around, so I find my acceptance in other men."

"My dad was there, but never affirmed me."

"My dad was abusive."

"My grandpa was abusive."

"My husband was abusive."

The truth is, we live in a sinful world, full of sinful people, and sin causes pain and damage. I have never met a person who was entirely exempt from the pain of another's sin. If I spent time meditating on how many people I know who have experienced unthinkable tragedy and undeserved abuse, it wouldn't take long to sink into depression and lose hope for this world, but there is good news! It is possible to move past our past and live our lives in peace, joy, and freedom, despite the unthinkable things we've experienced. I know, because I have met countless people who have done it.

Jesus looked at them and said, "With man this is impossible, but not with God; all things are possible with God."
—Mark 10:27

"She had always hoped to hear "I'm sorry" before she said her final goodbye to her mother, but that sorry had never come."

Tanya's Story

As she put her feet to the floor that morning, her heart sank. She felt a pit in her stomach as she remembered that today was the day she would lay her mother to rest. She'd known this day would come, but she could never have prepared for it.

She stared at the urn—the remains of the woman who caused her pain, heartbreak, insecurity, and fear. She had always hoped to hear "I'm sorry" before she said her final goodbye to her mother, but that sorry had never come. And although there would be grief and sadness in the following days, Tanya had no regrets. You see, two years prior, she made a commitment to God to forgive her mother for everything: the abuse, abandonment, entitlement, and the fact that she had little remorse for her actions.

Tanya had to grow up quickly. While most young girls were trying out for the cheerleading team and playing in the yard, she was cleaning the house, which was her only outlet for her emotions and the only thing she could control in life. Her mother had left her at the age of eight, and her father seemed to be more interested in the bottom of a bottle than his daughter most days. So, at the young age of fourteen, Tanya moved out with her high school sweetheart and started her life. Her dream was to someday have a family of her own and to raise her children with all the love that she never had. She married young, and the two of them build a life on nothing but faith in God and food stamps. Against all odds, they made it. Colby got a college degree and a good-paying job, and they had five wonderful children, but their oldest is their favorite. (Okay, I made that last part up.)

As you may have guessed, Tanya and Colby are my parents and some of the most inspiring people on the planet. They are living proof that, by faith in a living God, you can do the impossible. You can raise a family in love, even if you never had a loving family. You can make it out of the ghetto. You can have a good life, even if your past wasn't good. You can be the mother you never had. You can be the father you never had. You can break the chains of generational curses and live differently than the world.

There is so much I could say about my parents, but I want to share how my mother managed to move past her past in hopes of helping you do the same.

"She spent twenty years giving her mother what her mother never gave to her."

After years of neglect, Tanya's mother decided to come back into her life. She was ready to make amends, but not for the reasons you would hope. She needed help. She had been diagnosed with diabetes and was too broke to care for herself and her boyfriend, so she reached out to Tanya for assistance. I can't imagine how that must have felt for my mother, but she made a very difficult and noble decision. She decided to give her mother what her mother never provided for her. She gave her care, money, meals, rides to doctors, and anything else it took to ensure her mother's health and safety. In the later years, Tanya became a home health aide simply so she could be the primary caretaker for her mom. She cleaned her home, took her phone calls, prayed for her, and stayed by her side until her last breath. She spent twenty years giving her mother what her mother never gave to her.

How? How on earth does someone get past all the emotions—the pain, the resentment, the bitterness, the missed opportunities? How do you love the unlovable and forgive the unforgivable?

Tanya knew forgiveness because she had experienced it herself. She had made Jesus her Lord and Savior at a young age and she was filled with the Holy Spirit, which empowered her to do things that she could never have done on her own. Her love of God was so overflowing in her heart that she was able to pour out that love on her mother, despite the many reasons that she shouldn't. Sure, there were moments of anger and times when she hated her mom for the way she was, but one night, the Lord spoke to Tanya and asked her to give all those burdens to Him. That night she cried uncontrollably as she said the words "I forgive her!" over and over and over, until the peace of God covered her like a blanket.

I believe we won't know the full power of that forgiveness until we get to heaven, but I know in part now.

That forgiveness made it possible for Tanya to be the loving mother she never had. That forgiveness made it possible for her to be happy and enjoy life. That forgiveness made it possible for her to have a healthy marriage for thirty years and counting. That forgiveness saved my grandmother. Two days before she passed, I was able to sit with Grandma and pray the prayer of salvation with her. With a weak, shaky voice, she repeated those precious, life-changing words in front of my mother and I.

The forgiveness from my mother made it possible for my

grandmother to receive the forgiveness of the Father. So what is holding you back today? What relationship in your past has kept you from living fully? Who have you blamed for your shortcomings and misfortune? Regardless of your past, you can experience abundant life and freedom in your future!

Make a decision that today you draw a line in the sand. Today you forget what lies behind and press on toward the goal of the upward call God has on your life.

Scripture Study

Therefore, if anyone is in Christ, he is a new creation. The old has passed away; behold, the new has come.
—2 Corinthians 5:17 (ESV)

And when you stand praying, if you hold anything against anyone, forgive them, so that your Father in heaven may forgive you your sins. —Mark 11:25

Journal Prompts

Who have you blamed for your shortcomings? Is there bitterness or unresolved anger in your heart toward someone? Write down those people you are forgiving and what you are forgiving them for. Be specific, as painful as it may be. Seeing those words on paper is powerful for the forgiveness process.

-12-

When Your Faith Is Weak

*I need to see you here. I need to know you're in control. Though my
heart is torn wide open; I will trust. I will remember.*

— *"I Will Sing," by Kari Jobe*

*We are hard pressed on every side, but not crushed; perplexed, but
not in despair; persecuted, but not abandoned; struck down, but
not destroyed.*

—*2 Corinthians 4:8–9*

*T*here will come times in our lives when our faith is shaken
to its core and we begin to question the God we once wor-
shipped. Tragedies, disasters, losses and hardships will hit—
and when they do, we will have to know how to respond.
Will we allow these trials to steal our faith, or will we find
the strength to praise God through them? This is the challenge Pam faced in 2012.

On Thursday, July 14, 2012, my husband Brian walked over
*to a friend's house to visit along with another friend. On Friday
morning when I woke, I realized he had never come home, which
was unlike him. He needed to be at work at 7:00, so of course I
started calling him and he didn't answer his phone.*

I started driving the neighborhood and looking for him. I called one of his coworkers because I didn't know what to do. Within two hours of that phone call, I had ten of his coworkers in my front yard helping to look for him. That number grew throughout the day, as he was a firefighter. My firefighter family never left my side. I remember calling my cousin that lived nearby and telling her I needed her. I remember calling Justin and Mindy asking for a prayer chain from their church. Our daughter was on vacation with them. On Saturday morning our families from out of town started arriving to help find him. We split up and started looking for him. We went back to the house for lunch. We were getting ready to leave again when the neighbor's daughter ran over and said to my daughter, "My dad found your dad." Our family and firefighter family went running to see him. He had committed suicide. His coworkers jumped into the boat and tried to save him; however, the police told them not to touch him. They needed to make sure it wasn't a murder.

I remember calling Justin and Mindy and telling them what had happened. I'm pretty sure Justin was crying by the time I hung up the phone. When they got home the next day with my daughter, that was the worst day of my life, having to tell her about her daddy. They didn't just drop her off. They stayed with me while I told her.

I did lose faith. I remember praying the night he didn't come home. I asked Jesus to bring him home. He didn't bring him home. I remember being so angry and hurt that he wouldn't bring Brian home to us and would do that to me and my kids. It took a long time for me to get my faith back.

I did find my faith again. I needed to so I could help my kids through. I prayed to have my faith restored. I asked for signs that everything was going to be okay. I moved my kids to be near family. They hated me for a while.

There are days that I still want to throw the towel in and run away and not come back. We've come a long ways in four years. Our oldest is in college. Our other daughter will graduate in 2017. Our son is in high school. We have all moved forward, taking one day at a time. If I hadn't found my faith again, none of us would have survived and would be where we are now.

—*Pam Heidelman*

I wish I could forget that weekend. I wish I could unhear the cry of young Bri when she found out her father had died. I wish I could go back to the days and months prior to that moment and be there for Brian, to tell him how worthy he was in God's eyes, to tell him what an amazing father he was. I wish I could have saved this family from such tragedy. Even today, I wish I could take away the pain, the grief, and the weight of this loss from them, but I can't.

These are the tragic events that can affect our faith in a good God. These are the things that shake us to the core and make us question our beliefs. So where do we go from here? How is it possible to have faith in a good God when we aren't experiencing His goodness? Why do these bad things happen to good people?

These are the questions we ask when we're faced with faith-shaking circumstances. In order to get through these times and restore our faith, we must understand where good and bad come from.

The Good, the Bad, and the Ugly

God blessed them and said to them, "Be fruitful and increase in number; fill the earth and subdue it. Rule over the fish in the sea and the birds in the sky and over every living creature that moves on the ground." Then God said, "I give you every seed-bearing plant on the face of the whole earth and every tree that has fruit with seed in it. They will be yours for food. And to all the beasts of the earth and all the birds in the sky and all the creatures that move along the ground—everything that has the breath of life in it—I give every green plant for food." And it was so. God saw all that he had made, and it was very good. —Genesis 1:28–31

"After all, what is love if it's not chosen?"

Ah, the Garden of Eden. It was a beautiful place. A place flowing with blessings, and they were ours to enjoy. God made man and woman in His image and gave us the perfect place to live.

We didn't know evil, pain, or tragedy. We didn't know death. Adam and Eve walked with God like you walk down the street with your friend. Life was perfect. But within our souls, God gave us free will. After all, what is love if it's not chosen? What is a relationship if it is forced? God wanted us to love Him and choose Him ourselves, just as He chose us.

I no longer call you servants, because a servant does not know his master's business. Instead, I have called you friends, for everything that I learned from my Father I have made known to you. You did not choose me, but I chose you and ap-

pointed you so that you might go and bear fruit—fruit that will last—and so that whatever you ask in my name the Father will give you. —John 15:15–16

If only we had chosen God from the beginning and never allowed the enemy, Satan, to tempt us to stray—then we would be enjoying the Garden of Eden, and God's perfect plan, to this day. But we didn't. When Adam and Eve rejected God's instruction, they handed the deed to this earth over to Satan, and we see the consequences of that all around us: death, evil, tragedy, pain, depression, fear, sickness, suicide. You don't have to look far to see the effects of sin in our world.

If God would have allowed that to be the end of this story, what a sad ending it would have been, but *thank* God He didn't! He didn't want us to live on this death-ridden, dark and sinful earth forever, so he gave us an opportunity for new life. He sent Jesus to the earth to restore His relationship with His children and bring them back home.

For God so loved the world that he gave his one and only Son, that whoever believes in him shall not perish but have eternal life. —John 3:16

After Jesus's death on the cross, and resurrection, He ascended back into heaven, to prepare a place for us…if we will accept it.

Do not let your hearts be troubled. You believe in God; believe also in me. My Father's house has many rooms; if that were not so, would I have told you that I am going there to prepare a place for you? And if I go and prepare a place for you, I will come back and take you to be with me that you also may be where I am. —John 14:1–3

To this day, God calls His children—you and I—to change our minds and choose Him again. He offers an end to our pain. He offers to wipe every tear from our eyes and heal our wounds. He has given us death in this life as a gateway to an eternal life that knows no darkness.

He will wipe every tear from their eyes. There will be no more death or mourning or crying or pain, for the old order of things has passed away. —Revelation 21:4

This is good news, friend! This means that all of those tragedies are not the end of us! It means that we will see those loved ones again. It means that pain, sickness, depression, fear, and worry are transient troubles that have been overcome.

In this world you will have trouble. But take heart! I have overcome the world. —John 16:33

"We will experience life the way it was meant to be for eternity, and death will have no power over us."

For those of us who choose Jesus as our Lord and Savior, the future is bright! If we can find the strength to keep our faith through troubled times, we will experience the Garden of Eden again. We will experience life the way it was meant to be for eternity, and death will have no power over us.

For the trumpet will sound, the dead will be raised imperishable, and we will be changed…When the perishable has been clothed with the imperishable, and the mortal with immortality, then the saying that is written will come true: "Death has been swallowed up in victory."

"Where, O death, is your victory? Where, O death, is your sting?"

The sting of death is sin, and the power of sin is the law. But thanks be to God! He gives us the victory through our Lord Jesus Christ. —1 Corinthians 15:52, 54–57

So, dear friend, it is my prayer that you can look your trouble in the eye today and declare "You have no power over me!" It is my hope that when this life gets dark, you can raise your eyes and keep your focus on the eternal.

So we fix our eyes not on what is seen, but on what is unseen, since what is seen is temporary, but what is unseen is eternal. —2 Corinthians 4:18

You are a friend of God, a child of the Most-High King, and an heir to His blessings. Your inheritance is not of this earth. It is "out of this world"! Every tear you shed in this life will be wiped away and replaced with joy in the next one. Do not allow the darkness of this life to take away your light. Remember who your enemy is, and do not give him the satisfaction of knowing he has defeated you. Fight back with faith in a Savior who loves you enough to die for you. Fight back with a hope in a God who restores all that has been lost!

ABCs of Faith

If you have never made that life-changing decision to place your faith in Jesus and declare Him as your Lord and Savior, don't let another day go by! The Bible makes it very clear that there is one way to heaven, and that is through faith in Jesus Christ. It's not about being good or bad. It's not about going to church. You can be a good person who goes to church every Sunday and still be missing out on the most important decision of your life.

My husband Justin was a good person who attended church with me for three years. He had not yet truly given his heart to Jesus, but one day, in his darkest hour, he looked up to heaven and prayed the most honest, heartfelt, authentic prayer he had ever prayed and was overwhelmed by emotion as he literally felt God washing over his body, filling the void in his heart and making him brand new.

If you declare with your mouth, "Jesus is Lord," and believe in your heart that God raised Him from the dead, you will be saved. —Romans 10:9

"There is nothing this world can throw your way that hasn't already been overcome for you."

I am so thankful that our God doesn't make it difficult! New life is just a simple "ABC prayer" away: accepting that we have sinned, believing in our hearts that Jesus is the Son of God and died for our sins, and confessing it with our mouths! Once you have done that, you can rest assured that there is nothing this world can throw your way that hasn't already been overcome for you.

This life will never be easy. God didn't promise that it would be. That's why He's provided a new one for us. One day we will all be enjoying an abundant life, lived freely without pain or trial, walking with the Lord and our fellow believers, as Adam and Eve did in the Garden of Eden. I've already placed my order for a sparkly unicorn and some heavenly ice cream!

Scripture Study

He will wipe every tear from their eyes. There will be no more death or mourning or crying or pain, for the old order of things has passed away. —Revelation 21:4

In this world you will have trouble. But take heart! I have overcome the world. —John 16:33

Journal Prompts

What events or circumstances have tested your faith? What does Jesus say about those things?

-13-

The Secret To Strength

And they overcame him by the blood of the Lamb, and by the word of their testimony. —Revelation 12:11 (KJV)

When you are in the battle, it is difficult to see how any good could possibly come from it. Many of us get stuck here—in the valley between our former life and the life we had hoped for.

Maybe you've lost a loved one, and you're not sure how you can ever be happy again. Maybe you are in a financial rut, and you don't see any way out of it. Maybe you are facing health challenges, and you are finding it hard to enjoy life. Maybe the pain of your past is making it hard for you to move on. Maybe guilt has a hold on you so hard that you don't feel like you deserve to be happy. Maybe depression has you sunk down so low that you can't even get out of bed. Maybe your marriage is in shambles, and it's affecting every other area of your life.

I don't know what battle you are facing that has been

stealing your strength lately, but I know this: there is a way out.

See, I am doing a new thing! Now it springs up; do you not perceive it? I am making a way in the wilderness and streams in the wasteland. —Isaiah 43:19

When I find myself stuck in a mental rut and finding it hard to be positive, there are two questions I ask myself that always help me see the way out:

- What can I learn from this?
- Who can I help when this is over?

What Can I Learn?

Sometimes we go through seasons of refinement. It is not a fun place to be.

What is refinement? Think of yourself as a precious stone, found in the depths of a mine. When you gave your heart to God, there was a lot of stuff in your life that was not good for you. So, little by little, He began to help you strip that stuff away, just as one would do with a newly found gemstone.

"It is the trials of life that refine us, teach us, shape us, and polish us into stronger vessels for God."

Then comes the refinement process. The cutting, chiseling, and polishing that follows can be painful and downright hard. God is working on you, shaping you, chiseling away some things from your heart, mind, and soul that were not meant to be there. If you want to become the man or woman that God called you to be, then this season is essential, and many times, comes through trial.

It is the trials of life that refine us, teach us, shape us, and polish us into stronger vessels for God. I bet that right now, you can think back in your life to seasons that you would say were very difficult, but you wouldn't trade them for anything because they made you stronger.

What makes you think this season is any different? You thought you were done learning and growing? Think again! We are all a work in progress, and not one of us is going to stop changing until Jesus comes back.

And I am certain that God, who began the good work within you, will continue His work until it is finally finished on the day when Christ Jesus returns. —Philippians 1:6 (NLT)

Throwing Phones and Stones

I can still remember as clear as day the night I threw my phone across the room. Well, actually there were multiple times, but this one in particular was a turning point in my spiritual life.

Justin was out of town on business. He was supposed to call from his hotel by 9:00 p.m. You know where this is going. Justin happens to be one of those "glass half-full" kind of people. He doesn't really pay great attention to detail and always assumes the best. So when his phone died while he was out having an impromptu lobster dinner with his coworkers in Maine, he thought, "Mindy won't mind if I call her when I get back to the hotel."

Boy, was he wrong! As I watched the clock tick past nine, ten, and then eleven o'clock, I began planning his funeral. Certainly no man that I married would go this long without calling me and letting me know that he made it safely to his destination. Certainly there would have been a cell phone nearby that he could have borrowed. So, since he hasn't called, he must be dead in an ambulance somewhere, or lifeless in a hospital bed. If he had breath in his lungs, he would have called by now. But...if for some crazy reason he was still alive, then I would be grateful to hear his voice when he called

Or so I thought. Around midnight, my phone rang and he barely got out a "hey honey" before I ripped him a new one. "You would have been better off dead than calling me this late! What on earth were you thinking?! I was worried sick all night! I've got your whole funeral planned out! You might still need it by the time I'm through with you!"

"That man is not your rock. I am. Now go free him up to simply be your husband."

Needless to say, that conversation didn't go quite as planned. He apologized, but not without telling me I was a little crazy, at which point I threw the phone. I went to bed in

tears that night, and just before drifting to sleep, I prayed the wife's prayer: "Lord, please change my husband."

Just then, I heard the comforting voice of my Heavenly Father, gently but boldly correcting me.

"That man is not your rock. I am. Now go free him up to simply be your husband."

The next day I wrote down all the unhealthy thoughts and habits that I had created by being so dependent on Justin. I had literally built my entire life around him. Every action he took—or didn't take—affected me. It was clear that God was using this tension to refine me. As I continued writing, I made a commitment to break my unhealthy dependency on Justin and place God back in His rightful place as my rock.

Then, I called Justin back and gave him some of the most freeing news he had ever heard. I told him what I felt God was speaking to me, and he said, "Honey, if you can figure out how to do that, you will be able to help so many people in life."

Then I realized that this freedom wasn't just for me, and it wasn't just for our family. It was for many more people that I would meet in the future.

"Who can I help when I overcome this?"

Who Can I Help?

When I turned my focus from my own pain and frustration to helping others, I suddenly saw the light of hope in my situation. This is the key to finding strength in your moment of weakness: asking yourself, "Who can I help when I overcome this?"

I happen to believe that there is a part of you that wants to make a difference. Sure, you want a good, happy life, but more importantly, you want to know that your life means something. You want your life to have significance.

Well, let me ask you this: What kind of significance does a life without trial have? Not much. If you were to never go through anything difficult, you could never relate to people that have to. The best person to help an addict is a former addict. The best person to help a young mother is someone who has been through those early years of mothering. The best person to help someone through depression is someone who knows what depression feels like and knows how to get through it.

"For each trial you face, you learn a new way to overcome."

Whatever you're going through is not meant to defeat you. You were created to defeat it. And you will do that when you can answer those two questions: What can I learn and who can I help?

When I overcame an unhealthy dependency on Justin, I began my journey to a personal ministry that has led me to speaking at women's conferences and writing this book. I found my identity in the Lord. I found a new confidence that couldn't be shaken by men. I found a new purpose that was my own. I never could have stepped out into my God-given destiny if I was still stuck in that unhealthy dependency. I learned some things, and now I am using those things to help others.

And that is just one area of life. For each trial you face, you learn a new way to overcome. A new battle plan. And when you've overcome it, you tell your story, and it is by that testimony that you bring others to victory.

And they overcame him by the blood of the Lamb, and by the word of their testimony. —Revelation 12:11 (KJV)

Toddlers and Tantrums

I'll never forget a message I heard by Charlotte Gambill on battles. She said, "God trains us in many forms of battle."

It's silly for us to think that we are going to go through only one or two major battles in life and then be scot-free the rest of our days. And yet, when trials seem to come like never-ending waves, we can get discouraged and wonder what we are doing wrong.

That's where I found myself in 2015. I was a nurse, pastor, and mom of four young kids. I felt like I had done nearly everything in my power to try to be a decent mom, and I still dealt with daily battles with my three-year-old, Temperance. Who knew that a tiny toddler would have the power to bring me to my knees in tears and prayer? I'd always thought I was a pretty even-keeled, patient, positive mother until this season. It was here that I realized just how far I had to go. They say "a man is only as strong as what makes him angry." In that case, I guess I was pretty weak. Every day when she got home from preschool, we would begin a battle of tempers as she opposed my nearly every instruction. She would throw herself to the floor, kick the walls, destroy her toys, you name it, and I was completely at a loss for ways to help her.

This wasn't our only battle. She also had a hard time controlling her impulses, which meant we had to keep our eye on her every move, or we might be starting another neighborhood search party. I still remember meeting my neighbor Chad for the first time. I was brushing my teeth when my doorbell rang, and there stood this tall, bearded man with my little Temperance at his side. "Is she yours? She was at my house." That's one way to introduce yourself. "Hi, my name is Mindy, and I'll be the terrible mother of this neighborhood."

"I remember crying myself to sleep at night—exhausted, confused, and angry at God for not helping me."

We couldn't take her anywhere with crowds, or anywhere quiet, which meant we pretty much didn't go anywhere with all the kids. When we did, I was that mom who had her kid on a leash. Yep. Go ahead and judge. Not only was she on a leash, but she didn't like her leash, so she spent the majority of that time crawling on the floor, tugging at it, or trying to wiggle her way out of it.

Every night since the day she was brought to us, I prayed for Temperance's healing and breakthrough. Every. Night. And every day, I woke up to the same battle. I remember crying myself to sleep at night—exhausted, confused, and angry at God for not helping me. I remember feeling sorry for myself for all the sacrifices I was making. I remember daydreaming about a different life, one without daily struggles.

But there came a day when all that changed. My circumstances didn't change right away, but my perspective did. It was the day I decided to look for the good in the situation. I had had enough with feeling sorry for myself. I had had enough with being angry, frustrated, and raising my voice. I decided that for one entire year, I would learn everything I could about raising kids, and I would find a way to help Temperance be her best self. I read books. I watched sermons. I studied different diagnoses and how to treat them. I enrolled in a parenting class and attended every session for fourteen weeks. I spoke with doctors, therapists, psychologists, and experts in parenting. I asked hundreds of questions. I implemented new technique after new technique until we found the ones that helped. I prayed for God to give me guidance.

And one day, the Holy Spirit spoke to me. He encouraged me to listen intently to the way I was speaking to each of my children. Then I remembered that I serve a God who calls what is *not* as though it *were* (Romans 4:17). I began talking to her and about her differently. I began parenting her as my heavenly Father parents me. And we began to see a change. There were many things that attributed to that change, from treatments and therapies to prayers and spoken scriptures.

Today, when our friends and family talk to Temperance, they can't believe how far she's come. God has done a miracle, but it wasn't just for her. It was for me too. I am a new, stronger, wiser, and more patient mother today because of what we've been through.

And it was for countless other children that I've been able to help. There were a lot of things I that I never would have learned if we hadn't been through that four-year battle. During that time, it was hard for me to be strong, but when I thought about all the children that I could help once I learned these things, it strengthened me to keep going.

"Your battle is not yours alone. It is an assignment for you to defeat, by the blood and power of Jesus Christ and the word of your testimony."

Today, I volunteer with struggling children in our elementary schools. I give advice to other mothers who are dealing with similar challenges. And I connect with kids on a level that I never would have had I not been on my knees in tears and prayer for Temperance.

What form of battle are you being trained in right now? What are you learning? How are you being refined? What will be different about you when you overcome this? And most importantly, who can you help when this is over? Your battle is not yours alone. It is an assignment for you to defeat, by the blood and power of Jesus Christ and the word of your testimony.

Jenn's Story

Jenn is one of those people who makes you feel like a friend from the moment you meet. She can talk to anyone about anything and has a way of connecting with even the hardest of hearts. But in talking with her about her story, I realized that this gift of connection came with a price. In her early adulthood, Jenn lost of total of twelve family members within three years, including her mother, brother, and both sets of grandparents. By her early thirties, she had sunk into depression while attempting to be a mother, wife, dialysis technician, and source of strength for her grieving family.

The years of pressure and grief took their toll. In her darkest hour, Jenn hit her knees in prayer for the first time in a while. At that point, she heard God speak to her: "I can give you back everything you've lost, but you have to give me everything you've gained."

Jenn surrendered her life to Jesus and began growing in her faith and walking with God. She found a new hope, joy, and freedom unlike she had ever experienced. Jenn gives credit for her new faith to her friend Julie, who seemed to always have just the right word of encouragement when she was struggling. It was through Julie that God brought a miraculous healing right in front of their eyes. In that moment Jenn knew the power of God was alive and active!

Jenn has found a way to turn her pain into purpose by using her life's tragedies as a way of connecting to others who are hurting. She says, "When people ask how I can be this positive after everything I've been through, I tell them, 'Every time I see someone struggling, I am able to connect with them.'"

Today, Jenn is free from depression. She shares openly about her loss, struggles, and hard times with anyone who needs to be encouraged. She still cares for patients on dialysis and has many times been the listening ear they so desperately needed when they were down.

How can someone like Jenn have faith after all the pain

she's experienced? In her words, "The things that have happened to me weren't directed at me; they were to empower me to help others."

If you can see your trial as an opportunity to learn, grow, be refined, and build a testimony, then you, my friend, are a rare gem, and God will use you to bring hope and healing to the world! I thank God for people like Jenn, and the countless others who have allowed God to turn their pain into purpose.

Scripture Study

I'll leave you with one of my favorite scriptures in the Bible:

And we know that in all things God works for the good of those who love him, who have been called according to his purpose. —Romans 8:28

In all things. In the great, the bad, and the ugly seasons of life, God can bring good. It is up to you and me to find that good, pursue it, and proclaim it to a world that so desperately needs it!

Journal Prompts

What can you learn from this trial? Who can you help when you overcome this? What is the testimony you hope to tell about this season?

Strength Stories

Let the redeemed of the Lord tell their story—

those he redeemed from the hand of the foe.

—Psalm 107:2

Bulletproof
Barbie Scanlon
Mother of Five, Photographer

I grew up as the youngest of eight kids. Being the baby of the family, I was a mama's girl. I was always with her, right by her side. One ordinary day during my eighth-grade year, I got ready for school, sat on my mom's lap, and gave her a hug goodbye, not knowing it would be our last moment together.

On my way home from school, the bus driver let me know the squad was at my house. Our neighbor stopped the bus a block away and she walked me to my house trembling, telling me my mother had had a heart attack. I watched as they tried to revive her and then took her away.

This by far was the hardest thing I have ever gone through. It is very difficult to put into words the heartache I felt for many, many years. The house was so silent. I had to get to know my dad, who had always been present but usually more focused on providing for me than building a relationship with me.

I had a huge hole in my heart, and I tried to fill it with the attention and love of a boy. I made him my world and nothing else mattered. By the end of my junior year, I was pregnant and scared. My dad said I had to give up the baby or have an abortion. I refused to have the abortion, so I was forced to either get married or not have a place to live, so we got married.

We thought we had it all figured out. After I had my son, my dad regretted what he had asked me to do. He loved my little boy and spoiled him rotten. We were married about two and a half years. During our last year of marriage, we lost our mobile home to a fire. Not long after that, I found out my husband had not been faithful. We got a divorce, and I felt like I was going to have a breakdown. I felt broken, shaken, and labeled as a divorced, single mom. I felt like a failure.

This began a little wild streak in me. I dated around and soon ended up in a very unstable seven-year relationship. We started out as great friends but once I fell in love, he began to slowly change. Some of his friends had tried to warn me to be careful, but I didn't listen. The abuse started verbally—shaming, putting me down, blaming me for everything, and telling me I wasn't good enough. Then he began throwing things and putting holes in the wall. He could go from being kind to angry in a split second, then back to apologizing and begging for forgiveness. We broke up and got back together many times. We had two children together during this time. At the end of our relationship, he decided to leave. He had met someone else. I was hurt but felt relief at the same time. Months later he tried to get back with me, but this time something in me had changed and I stood strong in saying no. This did not go over well with him. He told me many times that if I ever dated anyone else, he would kill them and me.

"I turned back around to find a loaded gun aimed at me."

After some time had passed, he seemed to have stabilized. He asked if our son, who was four at the time, could stay the night with him, and I agreed because he wanted to see his dad. The next morning he called me, asking questions and getting angry, so I hung up on him. Not long after that, as I was getting our two-year-old daughter out of bed, I saw him pull up with a terrible look on his face. I knew something was about to happen. I could never have predicted what happened next. When they came through the door, I turned my attention to my son, who was clearly upset. I turned back around to find a loaded gun aimed at me. I was in shock but did not believe he would use it. Then he shot me.

Thankfully, my niece was there. She got the little ones out of the house as I proceeded to fight for my life. It was as if I drifted into slow motion, pulling, shoving, attempting to run away, only to be hit with another bullet. I prayed for God to save me and not let me die.

Finally, he had me against the wall with the gun at my heart. The only thing blocking it was my hand. At this point I had been shot six times. I was bleeding everywhere and feeling like I was going to pass out. I pleaded with him, saying anything I thought he wanted to hear, and it was then that he broke. He dropped the gun and sobbed, "What have I done? I love you."

He walked me out and tried to put me in his truck, but I refused, afraid he might wreck and kill us both. So he pulled his tailgate down, and I sat there in disbelief: shocked, bleeding all over, wondering where my kids were and why the police hadn't arrived. A neighbor across the way saw me as I pointed to my bloodstained shoes. She ran back inside.

Finally, the police arrived and threw him to the ground. The squad rushed me to the local hospital and then to the Ohio State University Medical Center, where I had exploratory surgery.

After surviving six bullets, I felt as if I had come out victorious, but months later, when I went back to the hospital to get the last bullet removed, I sank into deep depression and PTSD.

I didn't want to ask for help. I felt hopeless and broken beyond repair. Many, many times I sobbed and asked God why He had kept me alive. "Why am I here just to suffer and be miserable? Why did he do this to me? Why did he do this in front of our kids?" I thought. I fell into a downward spiral of drinking, anger, rebellion, and numbness.

I knew I couldn't live this way forever. I had to make a decision. It was either continue on this path, let the enemy win, and destroy my life, or realize that this was my opportunity to start over and live my life with purpose. I decided to overcome. I gave my life over to the only One who could fix it, confessing my sins, asking for forgiveness, thanking God for my life and my family, and believing in Him for something more. I specifically asked God for a man who would love me for who I am and love my children as his own.

"Rather than hiding my past, I use it to encourage."

God's grace is beyond amazing, and He heard my prayers! He sent me a wonderful, loving husband who has been an incredible father to our kids and has treated me with kindness and respect. God has delivered me from anxiety and depression and so much more.

I still face trials in life, as I've lost my father, brother, and sister-in-law since we've been married. But I know now that I serve a gracious God who is always with me. As I look back on my life, I see many difficult, painful days, but He has always brought me through. He has brought good from every bad situation: Losing my mother made my father and I form a bond through the years that softened his heart. Losing my home to fire made me realize material possessions are just things. Through the divorce, I learned to see myself as more than damaged goods. And surviving six bullets allowed me to bring hope to others by sharing my story.

Rather than hiding my past, I use it to encourage. Every couple months, I go to the local women's shelter to talk with other women and share my story. I have a dream of writing my own book someday so that I can continue to use my story to help others.

From Financial Ruin to Disney World!
Kelly Janetzke
Mother of Four, Pastor's Assistant

My husband and I have always put God first in our finances. Giving 10 percent to the local church was a nonnegotiable. But in 2012–2013, we found ourselves in a tough place. We had two beautiful children, a great marriage, a wonderful church, and one *giant* pile of bills.

We were not big spenders. We didn't even have cable. Life just got expensive. After a random increase in our mortgage, escalating expenses of two children, and mountains of medical bills, we found ourselves hundreds of dollars short every month. We slowly fell further behind, always paying bills just before the shut-off date and getting our mortgage payment in just before the next one was due.

It was stressful. It was hard. It was draining. I was working part-time at our church and my husband, Ron, worked full-time in addition to a part-time job mowing grass on the weekends and taking college courses. We were doing everything we could to try to make ends meet. We stayed faithful to the Lord in our finances, tithing first from every paycheck. We wrote out scriptures and confessed God's promises over our finances every day. We fasted and prayed.

It sounds great on paper, but it was a battle. An ugly, hard battle every day. Despite our best efforts, nothing changed. In fact, each week things looked worse and worse. We did our best to stay positive and keep standing on the promises of God.

Just when we thought we were at the lowest low financially, on February 10 it got worse. We received a phone call that our amazing pastor had very unexpectedly passed away. We were devastated. And that same day, we received a letter from our mortgage company stating that we needed to send them $2,400 by March 8 or our home would go in foreclosure.

"We had come to the end of ourselves and finally given complete control to the Lord."

I remember sitting on the bed with my husband, both of us in tears. It felt like life was spinning completely out of control. The heartache of losing our pastor and the threat of losing our home was too much to process...But then, my husband picked up his Bible and picked up the letter from the mortgage company and said, "Are we going to believe this (holding up the Bible) or are we going to believe this (the letter from the mortgage company)?" Then he crumpled up the letter from the mortgage company and threw it away.

In the natural our financial situation didn't change in that moment, but I knew that in the spirit it had. We had come to the end of ourselves and finally given complete control to the Lord.

The next few weeks were tough, but we had peace that the Lord was taking care of us, and regardless of what happened, He was in the driver's seat.

Then the miracles started happening. My husband got a new job with better pay. God miraculously provided the $2,400 that we needed to pay the mortgage company, and in May 2014 our mortgage payment returned to what it previously had been. The medical bills were miraculously taken care of. We were blessed with an amazing vacation to Florida and Disney World…I could go on and on.

It still blows me away when I think of how God provided. He didn't just give us a little. He didn't just provide the "needs." He did exceedingly, abundantly more than we could ever have asked.

Double Blessing: When Miracles Multiply
Bill Ischy
Father of Three, Business Owner

Our telephone rang at about a quarter to six, and the message that was left for us was from my best friend's father. He had called to let us know that my best friend's youngest son, Fischer, was in the hospital with fluid on his lungs and a 106-degree fever. His request was simple: "Bill, please put Fischer on a prayer chain."

But what God laid on my heart involved much more than a simple prayer chain. I felt God calling me to this five-year-old boy. I told my wife I had to go and see my best friend, Fred, and his son.

As I drove to the hospital, I kept hearing God say to me, "Take the cross and pray; take the cross and pray."

A wooden cross hung from the rearview mirror in my car.

So I snatched the cross from the mirror, and I began to pray as I drove.

When I got to hospital, I walked into the room where Fred, his wife, Fred's parents, and of course Fischer were staying. I hugged each of them and sat on a bed next to my friend. We talked for a while about what was going on with Fischer, and then my friend's wife mentioned how their priest had been in earlier in the day to pray over Fischer and how Fischer had touched the Body of Christ while holding the Holy Sacrament.

I knew now was the time that God wanted me to pray for this boy. I stood up, walked over to his bed, and knelt down next to him. I pulled that wooden cross from my pocket and placed it in Fischer's hand. I could not believe how hot his hand was from the fever. I told Fischer he could hold this cross and pray to Jesus anytime he started feeling bad, sick, or scared, and that if he asked Jesus to be with him, that He would. I then began to pray silently with Fischer.

I cannot tell you how long I was kneeling and praying. It may have been one minute; it may have been one hour. I truly do not know. When I had finished praying with him, I stood up, turned around, and looked at my best friend. His eyes were as big as silver dollars and pooled with tears. I knew then God was at work in that moment. I remember feeling something very strange, but I wasn't sure what it was. I then suddenly realized I was soaking wet. My head and hair were dripping wet. The sweatshirt I was wearing was soaked around the neck, under my arms, and down my back.

My friend stood up, gave me a hug, and said, "Thank you."

Then the nurse came in to check Fischer's vitals. When she took his temperature, she looked at the thermometer and looked at his chart and then took his temperature again. Shocked, she said, "His temperature is 98.6 degrees." God did something amazing in that room that night.

"Bill, something is missing in my life and I don't know what it is, but I know you have it."

The miracle doesn't end there. Two days later, Fred called me at work on a Friday afternoon. I could hear in his voice that something was wrong. I asked him if Fischer was okay, and he confirmed that Fischer was in fact doing just great. With a huge sigh of relief, I asked him what was wrong. He simply said, "Bill, what happened in there?"

I said, "God was at work." He then asked how God could let something like that happen to his son. I told him, "God did not let that happen; things like this just happen." But God did use it as an opportunity to reach out to Fred. He then said, "Bill, something is missing in my life and I don't know what it is, but I know you have it." He proceeded to tell me how he was feeling lost and unsure of himself and how he felt that someone or something was calling out to him.

Fred and I have been best friends since we were eleven years old, and we have shared a lot of things together. We have shared hours upon hours in our favorite hunting spots and days and days fishing together. We have shared in each other's weddings, the births of his three boys and my three boys—but I never in my wildest imagination would have dreamt that I would ever get to share Jesus Christ with my best friend.

On that Friday afternoon I was blessed to share with him about how Jesus Christ has changed my life. And on that Friday afternoon, my best friend turned his life over to Jesus Christ. I know now why God called me to pray over that five-year-old boy. The miracle of healing made way for a greater miracle of an eternity secured.

Peace in the Storm
Kelsey Smallsreed
Registered Nurse, Labor and Delivery

It was a wonderful season of life for our little family of three. We were living in a home that we had built in a quaint neighborhood. My husband, Thomas, was working as an EMT after serving four years in the Marine Corps, and I had my dream job as a labor and delivery nurse. We were enjoying life and every moment with our little girl, Olivia. She was just a few months from turning two, and I remember thinking, "I am so blessed to have such a good kid." She was the perfect baby: healthy, happy, funny, smart, and super friendly. No one could have ever predicted what was around the corner for us.

I dropped Olivia off with my mother-in-law on my way to work at the hospital. I worked with the doctor who had delivered her, which was nice because I hadn't seen her in a long time. We caught up, and I told her how Olivia was going to be twenty months old the next day, and she told me she remembered her birth. It warmed my heart to hear her recall the details of that wonderful day and made me feel lucky to have a child that put a stamp on another person's heart just by being born.

I left work around midnight to pick up Olivia. When I got there, she was sleeping soundly but woke so cheerfully to see me. On the way home, she jibber-jabbered about dogs and enjoyed a few late-night goldfish crackers as a snack. I remember thinking, "Don't get your hopes up, little one; you're going back to bed when we get home." When we arrived, I offered her some water to wash down her goldfish, and then she snuggled up to me as I sang her a song, told her I loved her, put her to bed, and then headed to bed myself.

I woke to a call from Thomas, who was on his way home from working all night. "Am I waking you up right now?" he asked, confused. "It's almost ten-thirty."

I remember being in disbelief that Olivia was sleeping in this late. I said, "I hope everything's okay." Staying on the phone, I went to wake her up. I quietly opened her door and peeked in to find her in her cute little sleeping position. I almost walked back out, but I noticed something was off. Her blanket was still draped over her the same way I'd left it the night before. I looked closer for the rise and fall of her chest, but it wasn't moving.

I still didn't believe what I was seeing. When I picked her up, she was pale white and ice cold. Thomas heard my scream as I dropped the phone. I went into nurse mode, checking for signs of any cause for what I was seeing. I couldn't find any evidence. I remember looking into her eyes. They were just as beautiful as ever. Her cheek was still so soft as I gently kissed her. This couldn't be my baby. This couldn't be happening. I shook my head and screamed, "Olivia, no!"

"Then I had this very real feeling of complete peace wash over me."

Somewhere during that time, Thomas hung up and called 911. As I sat in her rocker holding my precious angel, feeling totally alone, I tried with all my might to memorize every square inch of her. I wanted to soak up every part of her so I could hold onto her for the rest of my life.

Then I had this very real feeling of complete peace wash over me. I knew without a shadow of a doubt that I was not holding my daughter anymore. She wasn't there anymore. I could feel God telling me in my heart and mind, "She is in heaven."

As I sat there holding her, I could feel Him holding me. I felt so comforted. I remember feeling surprised that in the worst moment in my life, I felt peace. How could this be? But I was so thankful. I had never known so certainly that God was real, and He was right there with me.

Then the rush of people came, and my peaceful moment with my daughter was gone as they took over and began doing everything they were trained to do. The house filled with medics, police officers, and detectives. As I watched them with her from across the room, I wanted so badly to take care of her one last time: "Can I give her a blanket? Can I bring her a baby doll? Can I wipe her nose? Can I give her one more kiss?"

The answers were all no, as I knew they would be. But even though I knew my baby was gone, I didn't want to stop mothering her. They sent me away to the neighbor's house as they continued. When Thomas got home, he met me, telling me he'd watched as they carried her out of our home for the last time, covered in a white sheet. In his shock, all he could think to say was "Bye, Liv" (his favorite nickname for her) as he watched her beautiful long hair flowing in the breeze.

My worst fears had come true. Waves of grief overtook me, threatening to pull me far down to a place of darkness where nothing lived except loneliness and heartache. I felt like I could die, and I wanted to. There was no reason to live. If she was gone, I wanted to be with her.

I looked up to the sky. It was a beautiful October day. I remember thinking, "How dare the sun be shining? How dare the sky be blue?" But despite my sorrow, anger, confusion, and heartache, I could feel God carrying me through my days—giving me strength and affirming to me in my heart and soul that Olivia was with Him and she was okay. I took comfort—and still take comfort—in the knowledge that as her mom all I've ever wanted for her was happiness, love, joy, safety, absence of pain and fear...and heaven is all of those things.

Some people wonder how one can recover from an event like that. I'm here to tell you that it's true that grief is a life-long journey filled with peaks and valleys, but it's the strength and power of God that keeps you going! If it had been just up to me, I too wouldn't have lived past October 8, 2014, but God had more plans for me. He blessed my husband and I with so much love from near and far—from people we knew to some who were complete strangers to us. Hundreds of people came to Olivia's memorial service to celebrate her "big" little life with us. God blessed me with validation that although her time on earth with us was short, her life was filled with so much purpose and impacted so many around her!

"I want to shout from the rooftops what God can do for those who let Him."

We now have two more beautiful daughters, Abigail and Cecelia. I have a new perspective on life, and I cherish our family time. I don't get too busy to sit on the couch and snuggle with my baby girls. I feel so incredibly thankful for all the blessings God has given me through the good times and bad. I want to shout from the rooftops what God can do for those who let Him. In my worst moment, He gave me peace like I had never felt, and to this day, He is using Olivia and her story to spread comfort, perspective, hope, and thankfulness. In my line of work, I sometimes have to take care of mamas who won't get to bring their babies home from the hospital. In those times, I am reminded of the strength God gave me to survive the unimaginable, and I'm humbled for the opportunity to pay it forward by being there for fellow bereaved mothers—to share with them that I know how they feel and to offer support, love, understanding, and allowance to grieve however they want, reassuring them that God is with them every step of the way.

Even in heaven, Olivia is making a difference. She is still a part of our family, although she's in a better place. One day we will be together again, but until then, I will tell her story—the story of a happy little girl who made such an impact in her short time, and the God who brings beauty from ashes.

Changing Paths
Cara Posani
Registered Nurse

*E*ver since I was a child, I always wanted to be a teacher. I would play school at home, pretending to grade papers and teach lessons to my teddy bears. It was my lifelong dream. So when it came time to choose my college major, I pursued a degree in education. However, a few years into it, that all changed.

I was visiting my grandma in the hospital. She had experienced complications of abdominal surgery and wasn't able to breathe on her own. My sister, Mindy, and I went there to pay her a visit and paint her nails. Grandma Donna always had her nails painted, and we weren't going to have it any other way, even in the hospital. As we painted, Mindy and I shared memories of our childhood with Grandma Donna. We laughed and cried a bit, reminiscing about brighter days with her, when she would dance up to our front porch, singing Patsy Cline, with her curly wig and fancy sequined hat. It was hard to see her this way—connected to tubes and relying on a machine to breathe. She couldn't talk, but as we lifted her hands to show her the bright red nail polish, she smiled in approval.

We spent many long hours visiting Grandma that year, and I had gotten quite adjusted to the smell of the hospital and the ringing of machines. One day before we left, I mentioned to my sister that I would have liked to be a nurse if I could have handled the sight of blood. I had never been able to stomach it. Any time I had an injury or saw myself bleeding, I would get queasy and pass out. I never thought I could make it in the medical field. But that day, Mindy encouraged me to think about it. She was a nurse herself and knew that I had a heart to help people. She saw the caretaker within me and believed I could make it through nursing school.

"So with a leap of faith, I changed my major."

So, with a leap of faith, I changed my major. Through nursing school, I learned that I really don't have an issue with the sight of *other* people's blood, just my own! I discovered a passion for caring for people, and I graduated with my R.N. from Ohio University.

Today, I have been a nurse for over seven years. I know without a doubt that God is using me in the medical field, not only to bring physical healing to people but to care for them spiritually and emotionally. I have had many opportunities to pray for patients and family members, and I have seen the Lord work in ways that only He can!

I am thankful for the time I spent with my grandma in her last days here on earth, thankful to her for helping me discover a calling I didn't know I had, and thankful to God for giving me the strength to change career paths. The Bible says, "Many are the plans in a man's heart, but the Lord's will prevails." I have seen that to be true for myself. I hope that my story will help someone else see that as well.

Lifeline from Above
Gail Craig
Blessed Grandmother of Two

*I*t was a nice, casual summer morning at home with my husband. Our oldest child, Chris, had just graduated from high school. Our daughter, Molly, was fifteen. She had stayed overnight with her best friend. It was just the two of us at home.

Our air conditioner wasn't working and the temperature was rising, so my husband, Mike, went out to take a look. A few moments later, I heard, "Gail! Gail!" from the back of the house.

When I got there, I saw my husband lying on the ground, lifeless. He had been electrocuted. I later realized that my husband couldn't possibly have been the one to call my name. He was out cold on the ground. The Lord had gotten my attention to come to the aid of my husband. I turned him over and began CPR, but it was nearly impossible—blood was projecting from his mouth and covering both of us. The medics arrived and continued CPR as they rushed him to St. Ann's Hospital, but he had breathed his last. When I arrived with our children, we were told that he had passed.

It was a tragic, unexpected day for our family, but God sent us comfort through an organization called Lifeline of Ohio. They called me to ask if my husband could be a donor. I said, "Absolutely." That began a journey for me that would bring healing from a great loss. Through Lifeline, I found a support group—people who had been where I had been. These people had experienced loss but found purpose in their pain as they told their stories of how their loved one had saved the life of someone else.

"Speaking in front of people was never my strength and it made me very nervous, but I wanted to help and use my story of tragedy for someone else's good. "

The next year, my son Chris was playing football for a local college when one of his teammates injured his ACL. I found out that he was in need of surgery, and it would require a tissue donation. I wondered if it would be possible to donate my late husband's tissue to help my son's friend. So I gave Lifeline a call. They had never done a direct tissue donation like this before, but they were happy to do it. The procedure was a success and attracted attention from all over! My son and I were asked to speak at events for Lifeline of Ohio, and we were invited to the Rose Bowl celebration. Speaking in front of people was never my strength and it made me very nervous, but I wanted to help and use my story of tragedy for someone else's good. So I told my story, and I continue to tell it today.

Through this trial, we were surrounded by love and support from friends and family and blessed with enough financial aid to help Chris through college. Mike had always enjoyed coaching the kids in sports. He would have loved to have been there when Chris played in college, but in a way, he was. The next time Chris's teammate stepped onto the football field, a part of his dad—my husband—was there with him.

My story is not one of a strong me, but a strong God, who can bring something good from any situation.

Finding Jesus on the Devil's Path
Mike King
UFC Fighter, Founder of "I Am Strength"

*B*efore finding Jesus, I lived for myself and no one else. At the beginning of my Ultimate Fighting Championship (UFC) career, I was focused on helping others and teaching children mixed martial arts (MMA), but as my stardom started to grow, I lost sight of what was important.

I soon found myself surrounded by people who didn't have my best interest in mind. Drugs and alcohol were very accessible, and I didn't hesitate indulging in this material world. At the precipice of my career, I found myself aligned with one of the most caring families I have ever met. The Thompson family in Simpsonville, South Carolina, who run Upstate Karate, helped me get to the next level of my career. Thanks to them, I landed a spot on The Ultimate Fighter 19, where I competed with some of the best in the world.

Following the show, I was offered a UFC contract. I jumped at the opportunity but allowed fear of failure to convince me to take performance-enhancing drugs to gain an edge. By doing this, I let everyone down—my family, the Thompsons, my managers, and my sponsors. The day of the fight, my name was called for a drug test. I knew I would fail, but I continued to focus on the fight. That night, I was awarded a $50,000 bonus along with the fight purse for the fight of the night.

Everything seemed grand, but I knew what was coming around the corner. For weeks I waited for the other shoe to drop, all the while getting praise from the MMA world about how bright my future was in the sport. News finally came down that I had failed. I was suspended and fined, and my UFC contract was voided.

My life as I knew it was over, or so I thought. I turned to drugs and alcohol to numb the pain and consequently lost everyone and everything important in my life. From this point, I had two options: pick myself up and move forward, or give up completely. Luckily, I found my wife while visiting my brother in NYC. She gave me a reason to love again. This gift was what started me back on the right path.

After working a meaningless project management job for two years, I was still grasping for something more in life. I found that in Jesus when He revealed Himself to me on my journey across the Devil's Path.

The Devil's Path, an east-to-west voyage along the spine of the Catskills in New York, is often cited as the toughest hiking trail in the east. Over twenty-five miles, it ascends six major peaks, plunging into deep valleys between climbs. Honestly, I was a bit nervous after doing my research about what lay ahead. Backpackers hoping to complete the route face a total climb and descent of more than 14,000 feet. Most backpacking groups commit three days of hiking to complete the route, according to the trail conference. Backpackers can camp in lean-tos along the way and purify water from streams.

My friend, Brendan, and I entered the woods late on a Monday night, hoping to complete the trail in less than forty-eight hours.

On the first night, shouldering about fifty pounds in my backpack, I thought I had lost the trail as it climbed up the side of a slope. "This can't be right," I shouted down, one hand on a root and the other clutching a crack in the rock. I was lost. I hadn't seen or heard Brendan in what seemed like an hour, and my headlamp wasn't exactly doing its job in the fog. Plodding through the forest on a journey that seemed to have no ending, panic started to set in, but out of nowhere Brendan's headlamp shined above the outcrop. A light at the end of the tunnel. The glint of a trail marker sign sparked in the night, verifying our position to be correct on the precipitous path.

At that time, I did not fully grasp what had just happened. I just knew I was scared, and someone had answered my prayers.

The people walking in darkness have seen a great light; on those living in the land of deep darkness a light has dawned. — *Isaiah 9:2*

"I could sense God calling me—pulling me into something new."

The next morning, from the top of Twin Mountain, a 3,673-foot crest near the east end of the trail, I stood in amazement of the landscape. At this moment I started to understand what was happening around me. Our Lord was speaking to me, showing me my new path. Through God's creation, one can find himself and his Creator. Living in a city, you lose that connection because of the manmade creations that surround you. The atmosphere is focused on material possessions and self-gratification. I had gotten caught up in that way of thinking before this trip, but I could sense God calling me—pulling me into something new.

As we reached the top of the next mountain, I could feel my legs starting to get weak, and we still had four more peaks to trek. I was starting to question whether I had the strength to accomplish this goal. As fear began to creep in, I remembered what Josh Oppenheimer, a friend and business partner, said to me not two weeks before the trip: "God is love, and fear is the devil speaking to you." It made sense. The devil didn't want me to accomplish my goals. At that moment an inner struggle for my mind and heart began. Would I wake up every morning in fear of what lay ahead or decide to take and wrap each opportunity in love?

> *Finally, be strong in the Lord and in His mighty power. Put on the full armor of God, so that you can take your stand against the devil's schemes. —Ephesians 6:10–11*

"Helping people reconnect with their Creator through His creation was my new life purpose."

Tuesday turned out to be our long day on the path. We covered fourteen miles, including Twin Mountains, Sugarloaf, Plateau, and Hunter, all before nightfall. I went to bed that evening knowing I was going to be tired but excited about the next day's challenge. I felt like a new person. I had been touched this day by something I had never felt before. A complete happiness and sense of peace had come over me, and everything became clear. Helping people reconnect with their Creator through His creation was my new life purpose. It felt like He was showing me my future, and all I had to do was surrender myself to His will.

Wednesday dawned sunny and warm. A new day, and I was a new man. The clouds from the night before had lifted, not only in nature but within my soul. I cleaned the mud off my shoes and hung my sleeping bag on a tree limb to dry. Breakfast was granola and dried fruit. "One more big climb, right?" I inquired about the day's hike.

We had seven miles to go, including an ascent up West Kill Mountain, the highest point on the Devil's Path at 3,880 feet, but I had been given a purpose the night before and what felt like a new journey had begun. Brendan and I made fast progress to the top of West Kill, reaching the summit in less than two hours. The rest of the path was full of self-reflection and planning for what would happen next after I got back to civilization. I had so many ideas and hikes that were already planned from my adventures in the past. As a new man I had started a new journey with purpose through The Lord. I had been saved by surrendering to His will, and my goal was to help others do the same.

The Lord met me in the mountains that day on the Devil's Path and gave me a new purpose. He gave me a vision to start my current business called "I Am Strength," where I help people connect to nature and their Creator. The first trip is planned for July 23, 2017, in Kauai. My hope is to turn this into a foundation after working the business for one year. I am also in the process of connecting back with the MMA community and restarting that passion of mine, this time with a good cause in mind—using my platform and connections to help others.

Marriage on the Rocks
Drue and Meredith Gray
Kubota Manager, Founder of Meredee Designs

*D*rue and I met in the fall of 2000 at college. We fell in love and were married in 2003. Marriage wasn't always easy, but the one thing that seemed to help ours was good communication. We were both pretty good at sharing our thoughts, dreams, and concerns with each other and working things out. Our first ten years of marriage, we were part of a business team together. We shared common goals and worked hard to achieve them. When we succeeded, we celebrated together. When we came up short, we strategized together and tried again. We thought our marriage was pretty solid, but in late 2011, we encountered some significant life changes that would shake us to the core and challenge our relationship.

We lost ten loved ones in a short period of time. Some family, some coworkers, some friends—but all precious to us. This would have been tough enough, but on top of the grief, finances were impossible. I was a stay-at-home mom with our two young kids, so Drue picked up as much work as he could to provide. In addition to his full-time job, he picked up a third-shift position, umpired baseball games on the side, and took college courses to finish his degree. At this point, we were grieving, broke, and never seeing each other. He would come into the house exhausted, have a bite to eat, get a couple hours of sleep, then head back out to the next shift. Before this season, we always knew we had each other to lean on, but at this point, we found it hard to even have a conversation, and we slowly drifted apart. It got to the point where I wasn't sure we would make it.

I called our pastor Mindy and told her that we needed something in our lives if we were going to stay married. I asked if she knew of any small groups we could join. It was God's perfect timing. She called back and said, "Justin and I are starting a group with the Jenkins, and we'd love for you to join." At that point, the next step was convincing Drue. I knew he would be hesitant, because this would require us to let our guard down. He reluctantly agreed. It was outside of his comfort zone, but it was our last shot at saving our marriage. And it did.

"We found new hope that we could make it."

In that small group, through meeting new friends, sharing our ups and downs, and rebuilding our communication with each other, we found new strength for our marriage. We found new hope that we could make it.

Since then, Drue has completed his degree, landed an amazing job managing for Kubota, and was able to quit working nights and umpiring games. Today, we are more in love than ever. We enjoy our regular date nights and fun family nights. He still gives me butterflies when I know he's coming home from a business trip. We have a renewed intimacy and passion in our marriage—thanks to a small group of friends, and the God who brought us all together at just the right time.

Christmas Miracle
Amy Hardin
Survivor

*S*ince the day I was born, I have been fighting for my life. I was born with a disorder that caused apnea. Without warning, I would stop breathing and need resuscitation. At one point, they thought I had died for good. I stopped breathing for so long that after I had been brought back, the doctors warned my mom that I would have brain damage from the lack of oxygen. I was not allowed to go home from the hospital with my biological mother because she was unable to perform CPR on me, so I was adopted by two people I now call Mom and Dad.

"One mountain was conquered, but there were larger ones ahead."

In addition to the apnea, they believed something else was wrong. I wasn't able to do what other babies could do at my age. The doctors considered it to be muscular dystrophy, but before my parents informed the rest of the family of my diagnosis, my grandmother called with a surprising comment: "I have been praying, and I don't know what it is, but Amy is healed." And she was right. Something changed that day, and I was healed. One mountain was conquered, but there were larger ones ahead.

At age three I was diagnosed with nephritis, a kidney disease. The doctors told my mom that if I made it to age thirteen without any issues, I would be in the clear. But around that time, I started noticing physical changes. I would get tired more easily, and I also was experiencing urinary issues.

I've heard people say, "Your life can change in a moment." That is exactly what happened to me at age seventeen. I was sitting in French class, listening to the lecture, when suddenly I felt my heart racing. Then my breathing quickened. I couldn't catch my breath. I looked at the teacher. I could see her lips moving, but I couldn't hear anything. They took me to the office and called 911.

When the EMS arrived, my blood pressure was stroke level. As they rushed me to the hospital, I began to seize. The next thing I remember is waking up in Mount Carmel East Hospital. I looked across the room and mustered up the strength to say "Dad" before another seizure began. I woke up again, this time in Children's Hospital. The doctors had stabilized the seizures, but they had bad news for me. They told me I had been misdiagnosed. They said I had polycystic kidney disease and was in need of dialysis as soon as possible. They had never seen a case as bad as mine.

"I knew what I had to do to survive, and I wasn't going to waste time feeling sorry for myself."

I felt like I was in a movie—like this wasn't real, and I was watching someone else's life get turned upside down. One minute I was a teenage student in French class; the next I was fighting for my life in a hospital. But I didn't cry. I have always had the attitude that there is no need for self-pity. I knew what I had to do to survive, and I wasn't going to waste time feeling sorry for myself.

I was on dialysis for over six months. My parents got tested to see if either would be a match for my kidney transplant. Thankfully, they both were. Mom was planning to donate her kidney, but upon the final test, they found blood in her urine and told her she wouldn't be allowed to go through with the procedure. She was devastated, but God knew what was best. My dad successfully donated his kidney to me, and my mom was able to care for me through the procedure and post-op. What God knew that we didn't was that my father had been seeing another woman, and wouldn't be mentally, physically, or emotionally there for me, or the rest of the family, the following days and months.

After the transplant, I was no longer in need of dialysis. I got my life back, or so I thought. What started as a wonderful gift of a second chance soon became a topic of tension within our home. As my body began to reject the new foreign kidney, my dad took it personally and blamed me each time I had symptoms. He accused me of not "taking care" of it. At this point, I was trying to survive, deal with my parents' separation, help my younger siblings through the process, and be there for my hurting mother. It was a valley I would never want to return to. I wondered how life could possibly get worse, but I had already seen enough in life to know that it can always be worse.

Seven years after my transplant, the kidney failed, and I was placed back on dialysis. It was a rocky road from that point on. I was rarely able to complete a treatment without complications. I attempted an at-home dialysis option, in which they use the abdomen rather than the chest catheter, but that too failed and, in addition, caused congestive heart failure, with which I still deal today.

Dialysis patients are dependent upon what they call their "access" for life. This is the location in the body from which blood is pulled and then returned after cleaning. Most patients have an access in their arm that works long-term, as long as there aren't any complications. I was never that fortunate. The doctors and surgeons made every attempt possible to get me adequate treatments, but each attempt left me with another bruise, another hole in my chest, and another day full of fatigue and sickness.

One day a surgeon approached me with a hopeful option. He said it was called the "HeRO Graft." It was a new procedure that would connect the dialysis graft to an artery on one side and into my heart on the other, providing a means for adequate treatment—if it worked, that is. I went into the procedure knowing this was my last chance. If this didn't work, I was out of options.

I woke from the procedure in immense pain. I begged the nurse for medication, but she said she had already given me the maximum dose. I cried and screamed in agony. I had been through many surgeries in life, but I had never experienced a pain this intense. Finally, the doctor arrived. He took one look at my arm and noticed it was turning color; then he gave me the worst news I could have heard. He said I had two options: either live with the pain, and most likely lose my arm anyway, or remove the HeRO Graft and have two weeks to live. Without the graft, I couldn't have dialysis. Without dialysis, I couldn't survive. The doctors had told me that the chances of finding a kidney that matched at this point were less than 1 percent, due to all the changes my body had been through over the years.

"I had come to terms with my fate. I wasn't afraid to die."

I looked at my husband, who had tears in his eyes. We had just gotten married a few days earlier. I looked at my mom, who could tell I was tired of fighting. I told her I loved her and I was sorry. Then I looked at the doctor and said, "Take it out." I had come to terms with my fate. I wasn't afraid to die.

We began the process of end-of-life planning. Many friends and family members came to visit me. My mom took me to do some of the things I had always wanted to do. I went to a tearoom. I made jewelry. I took some of my most precious possessions and made sure they were given to the people I wanted to have them. I prayed for God's will to be done. We were all coming to grips with the future, except my husband. He boldly proclaimed, "You're not going to die!"

Two weeks went by. I was still here. Then two more weeks went by. I was still here. Then those weeks turned into months, and I was still living and breathing. I began to believe that God still had a purpose for me on this earth. All this time, I was praying. My family was praying. We were all believing for a miracle. As the Christmas season approached, we continued to pray, and that December, I was given the best Christmas gift ever.

It was an ordinary morning. My husband was getting ready for work when our phone rang. It was the transplant coordinator. She said they had found a potential kidney. And once again, I felt like I was in a movie. This couldn't be real life. I stood there in shock. I fell into my husband's arms and began to cry. After a few moments, I got the words out: "They found me a kidney!"

We went to the hospital, and the next morning I successfully came through my second kidney transplant. It was December 17, 2014—a Christmas miracle.

I was told that just a few days prior to my transplant, the laws were changed, allowing for people in Ohio to receive kidneys from across the country. If this man, whoever he was, would have passed a few days earlier, his kidney would not have saved my life.

People often ask how I am so peaceful and not bitter about all I've been through in life. I truly just don't know any other way to be but thankful for the life I do have. I have been given a second, third, and fourth chance at life. I have a wonderful husband and supportive family. The faith they had kept me going when my faith was weak. My sister was a huge source of strength for me when I was weak. She would send me scriptures, songs on CDs, and encouraging prayers.

Each trial I experienced gave me another reason to talk to God, which meant I spent many hours and many days in conversation with Him. My relationship with God and my family was strengthened through my health challenges.

"I find strength in my purpose—to give hope to others."

Lastly, I find strength in my purpose—to give hope to others. I have been able to encourage a mother after the loss of a child—reminding her that death is not the end, but the beginning of new life. I have been able to encourage those with health challenges themselves, reminding them that God can do the impossible, because He has done the impossible for me. I know without a shadow of a doubt that God is real because He has been with me every day of my life and made Himself known in even the darkest hours. I don't know what the future holds, but I know God will be with me through it.

Fighting with Integrity
Ted Pennington
Father of Five, Information Systems Security Manager

*I*t is a day I'll never forget. When I arrived home from work, I felt a weird sense of foreboding similar to the one a person may experience when the atmosphere changes drastically just before a storm. Everything was off. I felt stressed and sick inside for no known reason. As I entered my home, I immediately noticed things out of place, missing, and sorted through. The place looked ransacked. The feeling was so strong that I walked outside, literally to see if a storm was coming. Then it happened. While standing in my front yard, I heard a man's voice say my name. I turned around and stood there with the wind knocked out of me, as he served me my papers.

This was the start of a thirty-four month battle that would ultimately end in divorce. I had seen the signs coming, but what I didn't see coming was the war that was about to ensue for my life, my son, and my integrity.

Divorce is rarely easy. It usually ends in regret and resentment. No one goes into marriage wanting to be hurt, and I can't imagine anyone intends to maliciously hurt their spouse either. However, in the midst of divorce, sometimes people get desperate and try to position themselves to win. They compromise their values to gain possession of what they value most.

In the case of my divorce, what we both valued most was custody of our son.

This led to the most horrible season of my life. My wife

was willing to do or say anything to win custody of our son. This included accusing me of the most horrible and vile things imaginable.

As accusations were made, investigations followed. I couldn't believe what was happening. My first initial reaction was to fight back as hard as she was fighting me. If she was going to play dirty, then dirty is what she would get. This was how I had fought and won my battles in the past. However, this time something was different. I was different. In my past, I fought battles on my own strength. In the past, I used whatever means necessary to defend myself and protect what I held closest to me. However, this time as I sat there on the sidewalk with the wind knocked out of me, God gifted me with the His instruction to embody Psalm 26, and this scripture has served as the primary theme and foundation for my divorce and really my entire life since that moment.

Vindicate me, O Lord,
For I have walked in my integrity.
I have also trusted in the Lord;
I shall not slip.
Examine me, O Lord, and prove me;
Try my mind and my heart.
For Your lovingkindness is before my eyes,
And I have walked in Your truth.
I have not sat with idolatrous mortals,
Nor will I go in with hypocrites.
I have hated the assembly of evildoers,
And will not sit with the wicked.

I will wash my hands in innocence;
So I will go about Your altar, O LORD,
That I may proclaim with the voice of thanksgiving,
And tell of all Your wondrous works.
Lord, I have loved the habitation of Your house,
And the place where Your glory dwells.
Do not gather my soul with sinners,
Nor my life with bloodthirsty men,
In whose hands is a sinister scheme,
And whose right hand is full of bribes.
But as for me, I will walk in my integrity;
Redeem me and be merciful to me.
My foot stands in an even place;
In the congregations I will bless the LORD.
\-　Psalm 26 (NKJV)

" The Lord told me to walk out the divorce with integrity. "

    The Lord told me to walk out the divorce with integrity. Not to fight back on my own, but to allow Him to protect me. I wasn't to lie, manipulate, or scheme against her. I wasn't even to fight back with advances against her— only to defend myself and my relationship with my son. I was to trust Him... period.

The details of the battle are too much to share in this story, but I will say that at times it looked like I would never see my son again. In fact, at one point it was so desolate and the accusations were so numerous and so horrible, that the judge stepped in and removed custody from both of us and placed him in a temporary foster home for three months while they sorted out the truth.

" He fought the battle for me. "

Fast forward to the final day. The final verdict was such a victorious testimony to God's power and promise. Throughout the process, I had asked only for shared parenting and equal time. However, because of the false accusations and the erratic behavior from my ex-wife, the courts awarded me full custody and legal guardianship with 96 percent of my child's time placed into my care. I was so shocked, so relieved, so happy, so sad, so traumatized that I simply just fell to the floor. There on my knees, I was so overwhelmed physically and emotionally that I vomited. As I cried out loud, I clearly heard God tell me "your son is safe now". He protected me. He fought the battle for me. And it was His instruction to walk with integrity that proved to be what sustained me and swayed the courts in my favor.

The battle was won, but the war wasn't over. I still struggle to keep my integrity as additional accusations and darts are thrown my way. However, I have seen the faithfulness of God and now know the true source of my strength.

Today, I am engaged to be re-married to an incredible Christian woman, and for the first time, I am beginning a relationship with the same integrity in which I ended the last one. I trust God to guide me, lead me and sustain me through the ups and the downs and am so excited to have Him at the center of my life!

Your Story Here

We have each been given a strength story in life. We have all been through trials, valleys, and hardships that made us who we are today. We can choose to do one of two things with our story: keep it to ourselves, or use it to bring hope and encouragement to a world that needs to hear it. So, friend, what will you choose?

I encourage you to take some time to write down your strength story, and when the opportunity arrives, share it with someone else. You never know, it may be just what they need to hear to find strength for their life.

You can share your story with me at www.mindyross.org or on Facebook at the *Finding Strength* page.

Now go out there and overcome today!

Made in the USA
Columbia, SC
12 March 2021